Pagan Dreaming

The Magic of
Altered Consciousness

Pagan Dreaming

The Magic of
Altered Consciousness

Nimue Brown

Winchester, UK
Washington, USA

First published by Moon Books, 2015
Moon Books is an imprint of John Hunt Publishing Ltd., Laurel House, Station Approach,
Alresford, Hants, SO24 9JH, UK
office1@jhpbooks.net
www.johnhuntpublishing.com
www.moon-books.net

For distributor details and how to order please visit the 'Ordering' section on our website.

Text copyright: Nimue Brown 2014

ISBN: 978 1 78535 090 0
Library of Congress Control Number: 201593558

A CIP catalogue record for this book is available from the British Library.

Design: Stuart Davies

Printed and bound by CPI Group (UK) Ltd, Croydon, CR0 4YY, UK

We operate a distinctive and ethical publishing philosophy in all
areas of our business, from our global network of authors to
production and worldwide distribution.

CONTENTS

Dedicated to Nodens

Chapter One

Introductions

People have been interpreting dreams in magical and religious ways for a very long time. Probably as long as there have been life forms resembling people with ideas about magic and religion. What other creatures think about dreaming is anyone's guess, but it is an experience we have in common with other mammals. In some times and places, the dreaming life of humans is treated as important, in others as irrelevant nonsense. Mystical cultures are likely to value dreams more than those that pride themselves in being rational. However, being human and alive is not a wholly rational business, and dreams can have important things to tell us about even the most mundane aspects of existence. Dreams are very much part of life and, if we take them seriously, life changes. This is a book about how to integrate your dreaming into your life, exploring why this is such a valuable thing for a Pagan to do and considering how we might undertake to dream well.

Dream interpretation books abound and have come to dominate modern approaches to dreaming. The very logic of shoehorning meaning into dreams is something I want to question. Tomes written from the interpretation perspective will encourage you to pick static symbols out of your innately fluid dreams, and turn those symbols into a standard set of meanings, as defined for you by the book. 'Cranes flying east means bad news for business,' I recall reading, somewhere online. Such writing assumes that dreams are a universal language for which we simply need the right dictionary. We are to understand that the dream interpretation book is the right dictionary, and to trust it. There are thousands of them out there and they do not agree on much. Rather than opening us to the potential inspiration and

insight of our dreams, such narrow approaches to dream interpretation can have the effect of making dreams seem more tame,
banal and predictable than they really are. If we start with dictionaries of dream meanings, we can lose a great deal of the magic
and wonder, and will be much poorer as a consequence.

Rather than giving us insight, the usual dream interpretation
guides more usually offer cheap, disposable, meaningless noise.
'Today a man will lose his hat.' It is not unlike the ubiquitous
drivel of newspaper horoscopes; so generalised as to be
meaningless. While I do think that dreams can be interpreted in
useful ways, I do not believe that there is a universal symbolic
language with which to unlock this. I also believe there is much
more to dreaming than merely pulling a few 'meanings' out at the
end. As a consequence, while I will be exploring dream interpretation, it's not the only aspect of this book, and there are no handy
x=y pages for quick answers to dream experiences.

This is a dream book like no other. It draws heavily on what
I've learned from poking about as an enthusiastic amateur in the
science of dreaming, psychology, and counselling theories
alongside many years of observation and contemplation. Mixed
with this are the insights that come from years of Pagan practice,
which inspires me to recognise dreams as a spiritual
phenomenon as well as a psychological one. As a consequence,
this book will not give you glib answers about 'what your dreams
mean' but will help you to consider your own dreams and make
sense of them on your own terms. What I offer is an exploration
of dreaming as an experience that can lead and inspire us
spiritually.

It can be tempting to see dreams as purely something
happening in the mind, or equally to hive them off as spiritual
experiences totally separate from our waking lives. My understanding is that dreams can also be deeply rooted in our biology.
The more pressing our physical issues are, the more likely they
are to inform our dreams. In dreaming, body and soul remain

intertwined.

For those who see dreams as innately irrational, the strange, reality defying illogic of them can seem to be little more than foolish and whimsical distractions from the important business of life. This is not my experience at all. Having worked with dreams for many years, I find them to be very much involved with our waking lives. Often dreams are (admittedly distorted) mirrors we hold up to reflect on our waking experiences, fears and desires. We use our dreams to make sense of life. Thus how we sleep and how we dream has a direct relationship with how we experience waking life, both reflecting and informing it, even if we aren't conscious of that process. It is part of our life experience, and as valid as any other. At the same time I do not believe in getting over-enthusiastic about pulling out mystical messages from dreaming, although I think these too are present.

In the coming chapters, I will explore the dream as a pragmatic, bodily thing, as a psychological phenomenon and as a spiritual experience – these three aspects not being in any way at odds with each other from a Pagan perspective. As nature-based spirituality, Paganism invites us to root our beliefs firmly in the material world, and in personal experience. Dreaming is a very natural activity, bringing together mind, body and soul in powerful juxtapositions. We can reflect on the very real messages dreaming brings us about our lives and feelings. We may also find powerful spiritual experiences either through our experience of the physical, or in more mystical ways. I offer tools here for integrating your dreaming experience into your spiritual practice, and for using dreams to discover yourself as both a physical and a spiritual person.

True dreamwork is not about decoding symbolism or predicting the future. That whole approach is more akin to puzzles and games, more like solving a cryptic crossword rather than an experience that is essentially soulful. Dreamwork is a process of working with our dreams to explore self and soul;

learning, growing, deepening our awareness, expressing ourselves, finding inspiration, seeking the numinous and becoming more open to all that is.

Dreams have the power to give us tremendous insights, but only if we meet them on their own terms and put the reductive dream dictionaries to one side. Only when we let go of the idea of dreams purely as divination or irrelevant oddities, can we begin to explore their full spiritual potential.

My own background is in Druidry, but spiritual dreaming is not a uniquely Druidic activity. Shamanic traditions around the world work with dreaming, and the power of dreams features in myths and sacred tales from cultures worldwide. As a part of shared human experience, dreamwork also requires no belief, and is thus available to non-theistic Pagans, and to atheists. For the animist, dream can connect us to spirit. Theists may find reflections of the divine in dreaming. Those who honour their ancestors may meet the departed when they sleep. No matter which path you follow, working with dreams can be a part of that journey.

Interpreting Dreams

Having started by slating conventional dream interpretation, let's pause and consider the modern history of this line of spiritual and psychological work, and why it tends to crop up in certain forms more than others. The habitual approaches we have to dream interpretation exist for a reason.

In 1913, father of psychology, Sigmund Freud, wrote that psychoanalysts were 'able to some extent to translate the content of dreams independently of the dreamer's associations'.[1] I suspect this is the seed from which all modern approaches, alternative and mainstream, have since grown. Freud's influence shaped the development of the aspects of modern psychology/psychoanalysis that deal with the unconscious. While psychology and psychoanalysis have developed many branches and approaches, in the mind-body-spirit community we have largely followed Freud's lead and accepted the authority of the analyst/priest/author. MBS thinking tends to be influenced by what leaches out into the mainstream from all aspects of human endeavour. However, what this gives us can be fragmentary and piecemeal – such that practices and ideas show up stripped of their source and context, presented instead as 'truths'. It doesn't help us that Freud's writing taps straight into the archetype of Pagan priest as oracle and interpreter of dreams.

However, it's important to note that later on, in 1925, Freud wrote, 'Dream interpretation... without reference to the dreamer's associations would... remain a piece of unscientific virtuosity of the most doubtful value.' In twelve years, Freud's thinking had moved on, giving him a more complex, nuanced take on the subject. We are one hundred years on from his first statement, and a lot of other people haven't caught up to this second idea. As I write this, amazon.com has offered me nearly 2,000 entries for 'dream dictionary' and an even more alarming 22,000 entries for 'dream interpretation' although I imagine there will be some overlap. The titles and covers claim certainty and authority, as though each little book can tell you exactly what your unique and personal dreams mean. The arrogance of it is a bit of an affront, and the way in which this whole approach misleads and reduces dreaming, really frustrates me.

We know that our ancestors around the world went in for dream interpretation. We can look to the oracle at Delphi and Joseph in the Bible for easy references to the practice. What these give us are further examples of the professional expert, early Freud-style, making proclamations. This is not the entire history of dream interpretation in a nutshell. Furthermore, modern Paganism does not favour the authoritarian expert model. We are our own priests and priestesses, power is distributed and we all want the option of being able to do things for ourselves. Why should we accept the authority of a dream dictionary, when we would not accept the authority of an official priesthood?

There's an additional issue here that in ancestral cultures, interpreter and dreamer could be assumed to have exactly the same background, history, symbols and beliefs. A shared symbolic language makes it more likely that one person can meaningfully comment on another person's dreams. A glance at human history will show you that symbols are not universal. The swastika has been both a sun sign and a fascist emblem. Some cultures consider black cats to be good luck signs, others find them unlucky. All symbols are culturally specific in their meanings. So for ancestors who shared culture and symbolism, the priest might well be able to help the dreamer make sense of things. These days it is less likely that any two people will entirely share a symbolic language, making interpretation necessarily a more personal business.

We have a very diverse and fractured culture, exciting in its lack of hegemony, but in which we can no longer make assumptions about shared icons and archetypes. My symbols may well not be your symbols. Thanks to technology, we have access to a wide ranging culture that gives us new stories, imagery, metaphors and concepts on a daily basis as well as access to all of the available mythology and culture of the world. The speed and quantity of material we are exposed to also undermines our scope for having a shared symbolic language. What I read yesterday may inform me, and you have no way of knowing what I tapped into. The dreamer's associations can therefore be radically different to the ideas an interpreter brings to them. How can we possibly assume the existence of a universal language in this context? Furthermore, with such breadth and richness to draw on for potential symbols, how can a book of a few hundred pages hope to cover all possible symbols and meanings, or deal with the speed at which pop culture icons change?

Culture not only informs our symbols, it also tells us what is important. In materialistic western culture, we might be more motivated to look for insight into our careers and financial prospects, than into the condition of our morals and virtue, for example. This will direct us to pay more attention to some dream details than to others, and probably shape what we dream about in the first place. We are unlikely to dwell on things we truly consider to be irrelevant. Thus we cannot think about dreams without also bringing into consideration our relationship with our culture.

It is worth being cynical and considering that writing dream interpretations is really easy. You can make correlations with anything that takes your fancy, and no one can objectively prove that you are wrong. You might find it amusing and instructing to invent a few dream definitions of your own. Or, take some focus that pertains to the human experience (sex, ambition, frustration, depression) and work out how every dream you can remember having can be made to fit that interpretation. You will find that anything can be made to seem like a symbol of anything you want it to. If you intend to work with symbols, then understanding how innately malleable they are, and how vulnerable to our desires they can be, is really important. Any attempt at working with symbols has to at least try to budget in the impact of human desire – conscious and unconscious. All too often we see what we want, or what we fear may be true, not what is actually before us.

It can be very useful having the support and encouragement of someone who is more experienced, when entering the curious world of our dreams. However, when we hand over the interpretation process to someone else, we reduce our scope for insight and we miss out on much of the opportunity for engaging with our dreams. If you want to be entertained, a dream interpretation book can be amusing, but they do little to enable real spiritual discovery.

We can very easily tap into standard cultural archetypes when discussing dreams, without allowing for personal difference. This again is reductive and often produces misleading results. Parents are only emblems of support and protective nurturing if that was your experience of being a child. For the orphan or the abuse survivor, these archetypal norms do not apply in the same ways, to give one obvious example. Language can inform interpretation – especially around puns and double meanings, which is one of the reasons Freudian interpretations can look a tad odd in the English language. Our dreams are bound to be related to the language(s) we speak, and word play might well affect our choice of symbols. The slang, jargon and subcultures we belong to can all be an issue here, because language is varied according to age, and fragmented by subculture affiliations. Consider how terms of offence are re-appropriated and re-used by marginal groups and the ways in which new generations invariably subvert words. When I was young, 'wicked' was being re-imagined. 'Sick' has recently had the same makeover. We do not all speak the same language.

Mainstream psychology has moved on a long way since Freud, and aspects of that progress also manifest in MBS thinking. Jung, Freud's student, was publishing on the subject of dreams into the 1960s. He was a lot more interested in context and personal symbolism. Jung is also a key source for ideas around archetypes and the collective unconscious – ideas so widely held and repeated as to seem like established truths. These are ways of considering dreams and ideas – not definite realities in terms of how the mind works. Archetypes can be very useful for thinking about symbols in dreams though, especially when looking at the relationship between personal dream symbolism and cultural heritage.

The idea of the collective unconscious raises some interesting questions about how we understand the brain, the psyche and the dreaming experience. For many people, dreaming is understood as a way of tapping into something shared, a commonality of symbols, meanings and experiences; a sense of collective wisdom or potential. At the most biological level, we have brain structures that were created by evolution, in response to the breeding preferences of and survival pressures on our ancestors. Much of our mental infrastructure is very old, and held in common with other mammals. We could view the biology of the brain and the chemistry of emotion as a form of collective unconscious.

There is a more mystical way of understanding collective unconscious. We may see this as being like a plane of existence, an underpinning layer of reality, a magical dimension. It functions as a repository of knowing, wisdom, experience, archetype and symbol and is, in theory, accessible to all humanity. Envisioned in this way, it is akin to ideas of Akashic records, inherited memory and instinct. If you see all experience as present and available for us to tap into, then this creates a context for understanding what dreams are and how we might use them. It is not an interpretation I favour, but whether it is 'true' or not, is beyond me to say.

How we understand dreaming is very much a part of how we understand the nature of reality. Perhaps one of the biggest questions is whether you see the human mind as a discreet and isolated unit – a pre internet computer, or if for you it is just a box capable of receiving signals, and into which the whole wisdom of the world wide web may flow.

Jung also gives us some interesting ways of thinking about symbols. The Freud-style approach so common in dream dictionaries makes one item a sign for some other thing. For Jung, the symbol is complete unto itself, not a symptom or a representation, but a rich and complex form of expression. Most dream books tend to treat symbols as symptoms, as codes to decipher. If you can accept the symbol as a presence in its own right, engaging with it rather than trying to dissect it, whole other ways of thinking and working become available.

We are so used to being sold solutions that come in bottles, or other items that we are readily persuaded that such things are available and will work for us in other aspects of life, too. In our spiritual journeys, what we often need are opportunities to own ourselves and our experiences. When cures are big business, it can be tempting to sell us the idea that we are broken and need fixing, and then to sell us fixes that do not serve. I am appalled by the pathologising of normal experience for the sake of profit. I am equally revolted by the philosophy that everything we get is a consequence of karma or our thinking. I find the idea that misfortune is a consequence of negative thinking an affront. My own philosophy can be distilled down to the most basic premise that 'shit happens'. By making sense of our experiences, we can at least move on. It's not a promise of enlightenment, ease or fortune, but on the plus side, it does work!

So, to be clear, you are not going to learn from me how to unlock the secret of your dreams and then gain godlike powers over your destiny. You will not, after reading this book, be able to dependably predict the future, nor to unravel every aspect of your path. Do not expect to release vast hidden potential, magical powers or to solve your every ill. Nothing real works that way.

Most of your dreams will not turn out to be terribly meaningful. However, understanding the mundane dreams does lead to making better sense of your life. Most of your dreams will not be magical, but when you engage with them, they change. Paying attention to dreams is a way of reclaiming the wild, emotional, irrational and often wiser self displaced by the pressures of modern living.

Each dreamer is unique, and the process of discovering and claiming your dream life begins by not abdicating power. No one has the right or the insight to tell you what your dreams mean. Only you can determine that. I will share approaches and ideas, but you remain wholly responsible for the curious business of interpretation, where that turns out to be relevant for you.

Rather than trying to assert universal archetypes and shared meanings, what I think we have to do is seek out our own personal archetypes and examine our own, unconscious and symbolic language. We gain as much, if not more, from learning about our personal symbolism as we do from unravelling dreams. What are the symbols your mind uses to express to you things about your experience? Your dreams will be inspired by your life, family, history, community, culture, religion, nation, landscape, interests and ideas. Making sense of your dreams is very much about getting to know and understand yourself.

I am not a scientist or psychologist. I have not trained as a counsellor or psychoanalyst. I do not write from a place of intellectual authority. I am simply a Druid who has always worked with dreams, and I am sharing what I have. There is no dogma here, just ideas. If what you find on your journey is more than you know how to cope with, then seek out someone who is a professional in handling this kind of crisis. Not someone who will sell you meanings, but someone with the skill and insight to help you make the more difficult steps in your own journey.

What are Dreams?

While for much of human history we have connected dreams to spiritual experience, more recently science has sought to understand them in terms of brain functioning. We know now that the mind shifts through different phases of sleep, where there are different depths of unconsciousness. We know that dreams play a role in learning and memory and are part of the means by which we consolidate our impressions. If this is something that interests you, it's mainstream psychology and easily explored.

Sleep has a functional role for the body, practically, in enabling healing. The body and brain alike benefit from sleep, and sleep plays a role in recovering from mental illness as well as bodily ailments. Equally, poor sleep or sleep deprivation undermine physical and psychological health. Are dreams just a means to amuse ourselves while we sleep? A movie for the mind, if you will, to help us stay lying down? Are they no more than random noise created by the resting brain, or incidental to brain functions we aren't conscious of? Like most brain activity, dreams are hard to study. We might be able to observe activity in some part of the brain, but that doesn't translate smoothly into knowing what it means, or what use it serves. Otherwise we have to use self-reporting, which is notoriously flawed and unreliable.

In terms of the history of human evolution, it's worth noting that our cultures are very recent. Language, grammar, and arche-types exist in a moment of our history. Even something that seems as universal and timeless as motherhood exists in the form allowed to it by the fleeting cultural context of the moment. There's a tension between the immediacy of our culture, and the history of our species. We were 'primitive' for thousands of years before we created this strange thing: the modern human. Our evolution has not really equipped us to live in the habitat we've created. Our historic fight or flight responses don't work in our offices, for example. Dreaming has been with us far longer than the language we now speak, longer than cars and the internet. Dreaming pre-dates almost everything that we have deliberately constructed. It is a remaining pocket of wilderness holding out against our attempts at civilisation.

When Freud started taking dreams seriously, he was going against a consensus that viewed them as meaningless. The growing paradigm of reason had no place for considering irrational dreaming. Freud described dreams as coming from the unconscious mind, and revealing that which we try to repress. He was looking at the tension between animal self and modern humanity, but from a position that was not pre-disposed to think kindly of our animal nature. Dream analysis began in a context that wanted to tame nature – human and beyond. As Pagans, it is important that we remember this motivation when engaging with dreamwork. The process of interpreting dreams can be one of forcing sense onto them in order to make them coherent. This can have far more to do with the desire to rationalise and civilise, than anything more reasoned, ironically. As Pagans we can accept the wild, the irrational and the chaotic as part of nature, and we can accept that wildness as it manifests within us. Not everything is best understood through dissection.

I do think that repression can be a part of dreaming, but it certainly isn't the whole story. Repression makes a convenient narrative for rationalising the strangeness of dreams. If there are things we are hiding from ourselves, we can only raise the issues by coming at them indirectly and thus all the strangeness becomes easy to explain and innately less threatening. The glorious madness of our dreaming can be safely explained away, and we can restrict our investigations to some comfortably narrow parameters. What a waste! Rather than ascribing dreams to a part of the self that is more primitive, and by extension, less valuable, we Pagans have the scope to think about this in an entirely different way. Firstly we can reject the notion that 'primitive' automatically means 'inferior'. We are not slaves to the idea of progress. I suggest that what manifests in dreams may be wiser than the waking mind at times. The dreaming mind may be less restricted by the shackles of contemporary preconceptions and more honest about the various problems we all face in life.

I would also argue that the reason dreams are confusing and indirect will have nothing to do with repression most of the time. I think our dreaming mind is something older, pre-dating all this fixed language and a sense of objective reality. The dreaming mind is more flexible, and it speaks the language of symbols; not to hide things, but because this is its native tongue. In our waking lives, we struggle to speak clearly about emotional experience and existential issues. Modern life does not encourage us to think about feelings, or make time for such ponderings. Our dreaming minds have yet to catch up with this industrial, fiercely rational and objective approach we currently take towards living. We will be much the poorer if we do ever make that adaptation.

Our first task is to determine which sort of dreams we have. Are they rationally explicable? Are they full of Freudian repression, white noise or symbolic wisdom? The odds are that we all get a mix of these things. Some dreams will be easier to identify than others, but following sections of the book will explore how these different kinds of dreaming (and others besides) might be experienced.

All we can ever really do with our dreams, is guess. There can be no definite right or wrong answers about what they mean. If we use our dreams for self-aggrandizement, or to justify our shortcomings, we do ourselves no favours. If we interact with our dreams in search of self-knowledge and to enrich our lives, the odds are some good will come of that. As with all things, what you get depends a lot on what you choose to do, and what you choose to make of your experiences.

Personal Dreaming

One of my dominant memories from childhood is the frequency with which I had very vivid dreams, and nightmares. I was always an imaginative creature. There were dream interpretation books in my parents' bookcases, I knew about Joseph and his Biblical dream interpretation thanks to the musical, and somewhere along the way the idea of religious dream interpretation entered my awareness, too. The idea that dreams could be important, and could tell me something, has been with me for as long as I can remember. As a consequence, I have always paid attention to my dreams, have thought about them and made them a part of my life. Memories of childhood dreams are as vivid to me as memories of things I did when awake.

During my teenage years, I started exploring Paganism, and (largely through Neil Gaiman's *Sandman* series of comics) became aware of Morpheus, god of dreams. Later poking around brought me to realise that Morpheus is a complicated figure to say the least. There are no known temples dedicated to him, and no relics, no sacred writing and no artefacts. He crops up in Ovid's *Metamorphosis* as one of the Oneiroi – a group of minor deities implicated in dreaming. It is entirely possible that Morpheus is a work of fiction. However, when you're considering dreams, the lines between fiction and dreaming are especially blurry. The Sandman crept into my head, and has never left.

As a young person, I had no awareness that I was growing up in the kingdom of a Celtic dream god. It was while I was away from Gloucestershire that I became aware of Nodens, and only in the past few years have I come to consider him as part of my sacred landscape. His temple at Lydney (or the remains of it) is not far from where I live, so he has become part of my notion of place, and of ancestry in the land. A local dream god, perhaps the same as Ovid's, perhaps not. I do not speculate too much about the nature of deity, because it is not mine to know.

I spent a period of my life deeply unhappy with my life experience, my sense of self and options sorely narrowed. During this time, my once-rich dream life gradually reduced down to a tiny handful of banal anxiety dreams. It was a slow process of loss, and it robbed me by degrees of my sense of magic, the joy in my life and swathes of my identity. I've always been a creative person. Dreaming, daydreaming and making stuff up are intimately linked, and once that broke down, I was in crisis. I lost my inspiration, my sense of direction and so much else.

In the past four years or so, I've worked very deliberately to rebuild my sense of direction and identity. I have rediscovered important things that I knew as a young person, and then lost for a while. I have learned to do through skill and determination what I once did with grace and ease. The rebuilding of my life and the rebuilding of my dreaming have gone hand in hand: the same process, happening in different ways, each side of it enabling the other. Eventually I moved beyond the rebuilding work and, with firmer foundations, started to expand mind and self into new ways of being. I have used prayer, meditation, imagination and rest as healing tools. In turn, my dreams have become wilder, more inspirational experiences that uplift and enable me. It is all circular. It has left me very clear that if life robs you of dreams, it is essential to resist this, to escape, and to defend the self. What do we have, if we do not have our dreams?

While my experiences colour my writing, my Druidry has instilled in me a desire to avoid dogma. That something may be true and meaningful for me, does not, to my mind, imply that it must therefore be true for everyone. While I have brought a great deal of my broader experiences into the writing of this book, I have not shared much detail about my personal, spiritual experience. This is a very deliberate choice. There are some things that are too private to share and for me, the exact manifestations of spiritual experience are very much in that category. I have no desire to impress you with tales of my experiences. You do not need to know, and knowing might hamper you, because your path might be very different from mine. Your feelings and beliefs will shape and colour your experiences.

There are few things less appealing to many people than hearing about someone's dreams. I will go out on a limb and say that often, hearing about someone else's unsubstantiated personal gnosis can be just as irritating, if not more so, be it dreamed or otherwise. It is all too easy for this kind of material to sound egotistical; all about impressing others with how special and spiritual you are. It may not be wholly respectful to the divine, either, in much the same way that sharing intimate tales of the humans in our lives is not always respectful. It depends a lot on your relationship and which bits you choose to air. So, for the greater part, my personal spiritual experiences are noticeable in their absence. I make no claims for any magical or deity-approved status as a dreamer. I've just done a lot of it, and it is an aspect of life that I care about.

Ancestral dreaming

We live in a world of bright lights, caffeine and passable health. Up until relatively recently, our ancestors occupied a world with many more shadows and blurred edges. Long winter nights illuminated only by fires and candles. The normality of drinking alcohol all the time. The frequency of illness and infection, with the absence of antibiotics, meant that feverish hallucinations were far more available as an experience. Starvation, pain, injury... there were many more options for inducing visions and the world had more undefined spaces and mysteries in it.

Most of our ancestors had no street-lighting, and at night, the world beyond the home would have been darker, stranger and more suggestive than our illuminated spaces. In that environment, sleep patterns were different – two four-hour sleeps with a wakeful period between them. In those night time hours of wakefulness, in little or no light, how did our ancestors relate to dreams? I am inclined to think that the boundaries between dreams and wakefulness would have been a good deal less certain.

We have inherited so many myths full of magic, uncanny creatures, peculiar happenings... tales in which the reality of our ancestors appears a lot less fixed and dependable than the rationalist reality we now tend to think we inhabit. Perhaps the difference is not a loss of superstition, but a firmer boundary between dreams and wakefulness. Perhaps for our ancestors, the world was a stranger place, because dreams permeated waking life. Is our more stable and predictable reality more 'true' than theirs, or have we lost something?

In antiquity, books on dreams were numerous. *The Interpretation of Dreams*, by one Artemidorus (2nd century AD) is the only text surviving in full, but refers to so many other books that it suggests the existence of a broad, long lived tradition in which a great many people took interest. The prophetic aspect of dreams was of particular interest to our ancestors, as was showing examples of dreams being proved right. There's every reason to think that our European pre-Christian ancestors saw dreams and their symbols as being important parts of everyday life. While prophecy was important, there was also advice and instruction with more modest, day-to-day implications.

According to Michael Foucault,[2] Artemidorus was writing for everyone, and encouraging widespread dream interpretation. As the Celts didn't write anything down, we don't know how this compares with their approach to the value of ordinary people's dreams. Myths tend to focus on the lives of heroes, rulers and other important figures, which can create a distortion. We know that dreams and dream divination had a role for the ancient Druids; it would be pleasing to think that it wasn't all about the social hierarchy.

Dreams in antiquity served as a diagnostic tool for medicine, and to determine cures for physical ailments as well as spiritual and emotional issues. These days we are more likely to back up any dream insights with a trip to a more conventional doctor, but we have more cures, potions and interventions available to us than did most of our ancestors.

Ancient dream interpretation guides seem much better at recognising context – the life, status, intellect and moral virtue of the dreamer – and adding that to the interpretive mix. Modern guides tend to be far less nuanced, but no doubt life stage, wealth, health, relationships and education level will all play a part in shaping the modern sleeper's dream experience, too.

Chapter Two

The Body Dreaming

We are biological creatures. Our minds are cell structures and brain chemistry, connected to all the other cell structures and chemistry that make up our physical presence and enable us to live and act. Our dreams therefore can very easily be a consequence of what is going on with our bodies. Dreams can alert us to body issues we've not otherwise noticed, or were trying to ignore. Fears, beliefs and assumptions about our bodies can show up in our dreams, as well as more immediate physical experiences.

If there is a simple, physical explanation implied by a dream, that is the most likely cause of it. Dreams of hunger or desire most likely represent current bodily needs. Overheating during sleep or getting tangled in the bedclothes are classic stimuli for influencing dreams. Sounds permeate our sleeping minds, and can be transformed into strange echoes of the original. For example, I dreamed that I was struggling to make sense of a politician, who was talking utter nonsense. As I surfaced from sleep, the noises the politician was making became ever less word-like, until I woke and realised my cat was 'singing'. My choice of how to represent that sound in the dream may stand contemplating, but the sound itself is explained and needs no further consideration.

From personal observation and other people's anecdotes, I am confident that we can experience a very different relationship with time whilst dreaming. A few minutes of song played on a radio alarm can be dreamed through in incredible detail. We may distort other experiences, too; hunger may become outrageous eating, an uncomfortable bed can become a night in a torture chamber. Thus while physical experience can underpin dreams, it is not always the case that our body issues translate tidily into dream narratives. Still, when the dream is physical in origin, then the physical will dominate in the dream and there will be a fair correlation – pain shows up as pain, albeit in a different context. Sound shows up as sound, and so forth.

When considering this kind of interpretation, pay close attention to how you felt on waking as this will give you the best clues. Heat, cold, hunger and a full bladder are obvious, even when time has passed since the dream. The odds are such physical issues will still be with you when you wake up, or even later into your day. The value in identifying these physical cues is that we can make changes to improve bodily comfort, which gives us better quality sleep, and may also help us reduce or eliminate problems we have when awake. When life is busy and demanding, we can miss apparently small things that really do need our attention. The niggling shoulder pain, the small lump, the insufficient diet... taking these small things a bit more seriously can help keep us alive and healthy.

Good sleep, as previously commented, is necessary for good health. We don't just need quantity; quality is also vital. Our bodies will let us know if our sleeping environment isn't good enough. A cold, damp bed, a draughty room and noisy neighbours impair the quality of sleep. If your dreams are fragmentary, full of random, unconnected events, sudden noises, stops and starts then this suggests you are being disturbed. Check your environment and do what you can to improve it.

If our sleep is broken or we do not sleep for long enough, then we may not remember dreaming. If poor diet or lack of sun leave us with low serotonin levels, this will also make us less likely to recall dreaming. Repeated lack of dreams suggests that something is going wrong with our sleeping. That needs taking seriously because it has much wider health implications. It may turn out to be a mental/emotional health issue rather than a physical one, but this is no less serious and no less life-affecting.

The chemicals we put into our bodies affect our brain chemistry. If you do not like what happens in and around your dreaming for any reason, take a look at your diet, caffeine intake, alcohol use and drug/medication use. If appropriate, seek help. Or, if your level of concern is modest, just experiment with making some changes in your life and see what else shifts. Give any changes a few weeks to take effect as it can take a while for changes to work their way through your body and into your dreaming. Sometimes impacts from changes can be rapid and dramatic. If a snoring bedfellow is devastating your sleep, then a move to your own bed can have rapid impact, for example. Changes that result from reducing caffeine intake can be rapid as well, but improving nutrition might be slower to take full effect. More complex lifestyle changes can take time to have an effect.

If you are not sleeping well enough to dream you may have too much stress and anxiety in your life, which needs tackling at source. This will come up again in the dreaming mind section, but it is worth recognising that stress and anxiety are also bodily issues and affect us in profoundly physical ways. In terms of bodily aspects of stress and anxiety, you may need more exercise to help release stress, and if it is at all possible, change the situation that is harming you. It may also be an issue that you are not getting enough exercise to be bodily tired enough for sleep. This cannot be solved with dreamwork and must be tackled with lifestyle changes. We live in a stressful, anxiety inducing culture, so if this affects you it is important to be clear that this is not a shortcoming on your part. It is reasonable to be stressed by stressful things. It is a healthy, human response to be frightened by the nightmares humanity is creating. There is only so much we can do to tackle this at a personal level, but holding awareness that the problem is life and society, not us personally, does tend to help.

If you suffer from depression, or are temporarily set back by crisis, upset or challenge, this will impact on your dreaming.

Again, while some of this can be explored as a 'mind' issue, there are important physical aspects that need looking at. Exhaustion and lack of sleep can themselves be depression triggers. Poor diet can add to depression and anxiety, and create unbalanced mental states. Physical ill health can cause depression, and long term illness often does generate depressive illness as a side effect. Again, we live in a culture that does not prioritise health. Poverty undermines diet, excessive work hours undermine rest and sleep. Insecurity makes us depressed and anxious. Taking care of your most basic bodily needs is in many ways a radical act of political subversion. It is not easy to stand up to the system in order to protect yourself, but it is crucial to try to do this as much as you can.

Often we can refuse, or be unable to, identify mental unwellness. It is easy to assume that our despair over the state of our lives and the world is the only sane response and to then be crushed by a sense of powerlessness in face of all that is wrong. A loss of hope can eat away the foundations of your life without ever making itself apparent. Taking good care of your physical wellbeing can be a tool for overcoming, or at least mitigating, depression. Being alert to the quality and nature of our dreaming can help us identify when something is wrong, which can in turn make it easier to acknowledge when something is wrong with how we feel.

Short term dream problems can more easily be linked to immediate problems, or excess. Too much excitement can be as much of an unbalancer of dreams as tragedy. Both impact on our body chemistry. Longer term problems can be ignored in waking life and may become visible through dreaming problems. While dreamwork can be used productively around both long and short term challenges, this is not a magic solution for ills. If there are problems in your life, most often they will require action in your waking life as well to sort things out. It can be tempting to use Pagan and esoteric approaches to offset the woes of modern living. Meditating, praying, using physical disciplines and ritual, we make the unbearable tolerable. This is, I think, a mistake. We need to be making changes in our lives and in the world, not using our Paganism in self defence – that makes us complicit in all that is wrong.

While it can be useful to define issues through dreams, when there is a bodily problem, dreams cannot resolve your difficulties. Dreamwork for the purposes of reflection and insight can be productive, and working with dreams can help identify ways forward. However, for this to be useful, it is necessary to take the insights of dreamwork back to your body, your life and your waking experiences and make whatever changes are needed.

If your body is well, fit, relaxed for sleep, reasonably stress-free and allowed to rest in a suitable space, your dreams are less likely to be concerned with bodily issues. You can, to a degree, use your dreams to monitor your body and you may be able to spot problems early by this means. For example, I'm a vegetarian but will dream about eating meat if I've not had enough protein for a few days. It's a very simple way of my body expressing a need that I might not otherwise notice.

When our bodies are in good condition, there is room for the dreaming mind to consider other issues. Our emotional wellbeing will then be more apparent. As emotions are more complex to make sense of than purely mechanical body issues, I shall be working through them in more detail in the coming sections. If emotional needs are highly pressing, they may show through in dreams even when there are physical problems too. However, it is worth noting that emotions are all about body chemistry, and not separate from biology. I've also separated learning into a section about rational dreaming – again the body learns, but as this is more complex than considering our immediate physical needs I've created divisions for the sake of clarity. Everything we do as dreamers, we do in our bodies. It is the level of bodily engagement that we often need to figure out.

Here's a list (not exhaustive) of features that might suggest you have had a more mechanical bodily dream.

- Excessive or unusual consumption of food and drink, or substitutes for food and drink.
- Searching in vain for food or drink.
- A need to urinate/defecate, or actually doing either in the dream.
- Sexual activity, including troubling or inappropriate behaviour.
- Any dream content suggesting extreme temperatures – exaggerated heat or cold.
- Sound intrusions incompatible with the rest of the dream content.
- Dreaming you are in pain or being harmed in some bodily way.
- Falling, sudden jolts, disjointed stories.
- Dreams focused on physical activity – anything occurring intensively and becoming the dominant feature of a dream.

There can be other explanations for any of these dreams. If the physical activity seems incidental to the dream, then it probably isn't that important. If it seems like a plot device, it probably is nothing more than moving your story on. Whatever feels like the most important feature of the dream, is the most important feature. If the symbolism of your dream seems convoluted and is hard to decipher, the odds are this isn't a body dream at all – unless there are things relating to your body that you are reluctant to think about.

Your dreaming mind and your body evolved together and make sense to each other. No complex metaphors are needed to try to handle an idea like 'my bladder is full'. Complex body dreams are more likely to be about your emotional relationship with your own body and may be better considered in more emotional terms.

The Pineal Gland

In terms of physical structures associated with dreaming, the pineal gland appears to be critical. This small, pine-cone shaped gland inside the brain responds to changing light levels, releasing melatonin in order to regulate sleep and circadian rhythms. It also has an involvement with the metabolism, which may in turn underpin the connection between sleep deprivation and weight gain.

The pineal gland enables us to change levels of consciousness, which aside from giving it an important role in sleeping probably also means it is implicated in our capacity for spiritual experience. Some thinkers have imagined it to be the physical seat of the soul, while in modern New Age thinking it can be designated as a literal location for the third eye. The issue of light sensitivity and consciousness changing makes this an interesting interpretation. If you feel this is a helpful approach to your biology and consciousness, there is a wealth of information online that will tell you how it can be explored.

Over time, the pineal gland calcifies in many people. There doesn't seem to be much clarity, at the time of writing, over the implications for consciousness. Anecdotally speaking, the elderly often seem to need less sleep, and these things may be related. There is a school of thought that holds exposure to fluoride responsible for calcification of the pineal gland, and sometimes by extension, the closing of the third eye. Suggestions have also been made that it might have a role in Alzheimer's disease. As calcium can also show up in the pineal gland, this clearly isn't quite so simple an issue, but there are plenty of reasons to be wary of fluoride as it is. There may well be an important correlation between fluoride and calcification, but that does not establish causality, and there may be other chemicals or mechanisms in the mix, too.

I've not seen any wildly exciting New Age approaches to healing and cleansing the pineal gland – reduced alcohol intake and smoking less, reduced meat intake, health lifestyle – all the usual suspects for basic good health in fact, with the curious addition of being positive about raw chocolate. It may be early days in our understanding, rational and magical, of how to work with this part of ourselves.

Perhaps the one lesson to take from all of this is that our bodies and experiences are fragile. A small shift of diet, chemical exposure or artificial light changes us. So much of what we experience comes back to delicate systems of chemical interactions, and we should not be complacent about this. Modern humans enthusiastically construct living experiences that expose us to all manner of things we haven't evolved to cope with. We regularly encounter chemicals in quantities and combinations that we did not evolve to handle. Our minds and our consciousness are not unassailable or inevitable. We do not really know how we are being changed by the great unregulated, barely monitored and unplanned experiments we are currently carrying out upon ourselves in the name of progress and modernity.

Sleep Dysfunction

Being sleep deprived has a very direct and immediate impact on body and mind alike. Even one poor night of sleep undermines concentration and emotional wellbeing. A few nights with reduced sleep can result in weight gain, increased stress and impacts on decision-making abilities. Lack of sleep reduces our ability to learn. Longer term deprivation affects physical health, reduces our ability to heal and recover and can, in extremis, lead to hallucinations with consequences comparable (I understand, but not from personal experience!) to dropping acid.

We are clearly designed to be able to cope with broken sleep and the odd night of sleeplessness, but are not equipped to handle this if it continues beyond a few nights.

Oversleeping is a problem often associated with depressive illness and fatigue illness. Thus sometimes, people showing signs of depression will be encouraged to avoid the habit of sleeping a lot of their time. The dominant theory seems to be that sleeping longer locks you into patterns of inactivity that reinforce feelings of powerlessness and realities of nothing happening, which in turn helps you stay depressed. I have no doubt this will be true for some people. For others, sleep is not the cause of problems, but a way of dealing with emotional distress. We have a dominant medical perspective that tends to equate the suppression of symptoms with 'cure' and which will, therefore, deal with the symptom of excessive sleep, not the reason or the need for it.

I start from the assumption that sleep is a good, natural and health giving thing and if you want more of it, this is probably because you need more sleep. However, be aware that there are other situations a person can find themselves in, and if you are developing a habit of excessive sleep as a substitute for life, this is not generally considered to be in your interests.

Sometimes sleep deprivation is a consequence of life – small children, personal health issues, terrifying deadlines, cavorting at festivals and seeking sleep deprived spiritual experiences. When you've got one of these, you tend to know about it. This kind of issue is usually short term, and has an endpoint, although sleepless children can takes years, in worst case scenarios. Accepting sleep deprivation on these terms is something most of us do from time to time. These are perfectly reasonable choices to make – just don't attempt to live like it permanently, because it will eventually undermine your mental and physical health.

Insomnia is a sleep disturbance that is often harder to explain and is consequently a lot harder to either resolve or tolerate. When you know perfectly well why you're awake and exhausted, it is a good deal easier to bear than these occasions of your body failing to do what it should for no obvious reason at all.

I think there are three ways in which insomnia can strike – and there are often very different reasons underpinning the three forms.

1. Not being able to settle and sleep, either at all, or for enough of the night for it to result in sleep deprivation. This can be caused by caffeine intake, an over-active mind, a body that isn't tired enough, being emotionally unsettled, being over-exposed to light, over stimulated, having non-restful associations with the sleep space, being in an unfamiliar place, and having usual routines disrupted.

2. Waking in the night. We can, as part of normal sleeping patterns, surface from sleep, deal with bodily issues or minor disturbances and then go back to sleep with no ill effects. However, if on waking we can't resettle, this might not be a problem at all, but might be a pre-industrial sleep pattern reasserting itself (more on this later). If you can stay calm and go with it, being awake for an hour or two in the night need not be a problem and can be an asset. Persistent intrusions of light, sound or other sources of stress and disturbance may wake us up and then keep us awake. If it's subtle it can be hard to identify in a tired state. Full moons can cause problems in this way. An exhausted person may fall asleep despite environmental problems and then wake later because of them. This may result in being awake for some hours before being able to go back to sleep.

3. Waking early. This can be the consequence of being in tune with the light, and during the shortest nights of the year, can significantly impact on how much sleep you get. An overactive mind may work on problems during the night and wake you early to get busy on enacting the solutions come up with while asleep. Stress, anxiety, the demands of the day

ahead, and fear of oversleeping may also play a role. You can be exhausted enough to fall asleep but mentally or emotionally too disturbed to stay there for as long as you really need.

It isn't always obvious what's going wrong, or why. Being wakeful and distressed is not the best time to start asking what the problem is. If it isn't obvious why you aren't sleeping, it is better to ponder this when the issue is less pressing. In terms of unhelpful things to do late at night, poking around your own psyche for explanations certainly makes the list...

Here are some things which may be helpful:

- If there is an identifiable cause, tackle it. That sounds like obvious common sense, but all too often we are not sufficiently strident in tackling things harming our sleep. Asking someone else to respect your need for sleep can be especially problematic. Dealing with noise and light pollution can require significant interventions. Sorting out the fears that keep you awake isn't always easy, but it is the only thing that will reliably work if this is keeping you awake.
- Try to get more exposure to natural light and natural darkness. Our brain chemistry can go awry, especially if we get up in the dark for work and stay up with electric lights and this can throw out our natural sleeping rhythms.
- If you can't sleep, don't just lie there, do something! Meditate, or pray if that helps you stay in bed. Get up and move around. It is better to put a light on and read for a while than lie in the darkness and become distressed. You may be able to settle later, and will be better able to do so if you can avoid the insomnia having an emotional impact.
- Some people have more creative energy late at night. Try

working with the insomnia and see if it is something else trying to happen.

- If you can't sleep at night, try to make time to nap and catch up when you can. You may get some issues with sleep patterns by doing this, but a round of staying awake until it is dark and you are tired, and then sleeping, will tend to reset you.
- Medicinal drugs and alcohol may provide short term relief, but are not an answer. Unless you have a chemical imbalance, all you are doing is suppressing symptoms and letting the underlying issues continue.

Sometimes it won't be clear what the problem is, much less what would help resolve it. However, the more you do to take care of mental, emotional and physical health the rest of the time, the better. In my own life I have noticed that while there isn't always a direct correlation between when I'm most stressed and when I can't sleep, periods of high stress and periods of sleeplessness tend to coincide. If I don't get enough quiet down time, rest and exercise, the chances of my getting insomnia increase. I suspect that, often, it is a symptom of not looking after ourselves well enough the rest of the time, where it isn't a consequence of having rhythms out of synch with the clock.

From personal observation and the reporting of people I know, the biggest problem with sleep deprivation is not the physical impact. We can weather the tiredness, and the reduced functionality, and in the normal scheme of things will catch up later. The problem with insomnia is the emotional impact it has. This can start at the first signs of sleeplessness – the realisation that you are ruining the next day by not being able to sleep now. Being the only person awake late at night is lonely and isolating, and it is not for nothing that a spiritual crisis is often called 'a dark night of the soul'.

For anyone depressive, this can be the time when suicidal

thoughts sing their most alluring siren songs. Being alone in the dark, with no prospect of dawn or sleep can open us to all the darkest thoughts we carry. Then, that experience of distressed sleeplessness means the bed ceases to seem quite so safe, and becomes a place of waking nightmares, and this helps us stay unsettled for nights to come.

The most important thing to do when facing insomnia is to avoid taking emotional damage from it. Anything that works for you without hurting anyone else is worth exploring. Do whatever it takes not just to get through the darkness, but to get through calmly. It is not a personal failing. It is not a disaster. It is not you being stupid, or useless, or any of the other words of self-assault that may come up in the dark hours. It is not insufficiency. And even if it is your fault for drinking a pint of coffee, that still doesn't make you any kind of bad person. It's just a thing that is happening, but because of how much more emotionally open we can be when alone at night, it can seem like all those things and worse. If you can get through it calmly, you can stop it from becoming a serious problem for you. If you are calm, it's just sleep deprivation and a nuisance. If you become distressed, then you really do have a problem. Take good care of yourself, and have strategies for coping if it happens a lot, and you can, I promise, make it less traumatic at the very least.

I've experienced issues of insomnia intermittently through my whole life. There are many things in this book designed to help with good sleeping and avoiding the issue in the first place. Anything offered here has been tested extensively!

Rational Dreaming

There is a theory that much of what happens when we dream relates to the processes of memory within the brain. Most of us do not remember every detail of every day we have lived. Anything we do regularly will often be held as a generic memory, not lots of near identical, specific ones. Somewhere between the experience and the recollection, a process occurs. We sift and sort. Some things are forgotten. Other experiences become generic memories. Some things are preserved fairly accurately and in detail. How and when does this happen? How do we make the choices about what happens to our memories? It's clearly not a random process, because we remember important stuff and forget trivia, mostly. We can also suppress trauma by forgetting it. One possible answer to when and how we do this, is that it happens when we dream, or that our dreams are a side effect of the process.

Studies of how people learn have established that sleep plays an important part in this, too. There's only so far repetition and study will take you. You progress more effectively in any kind of learning process by stopping, resting and sleeping so that your mind can consolidate what's been learned. As an amateur musician I've observed this repeatedly. It's not during the regular practise that I make most progress, but the gaps between the practises. Our sifting process and the way in which we lay down memory is clearly related to learning, and it's often relevant to think about what we remember in terms of what we learn. Oft repeated experiences aren't teaching us much so we don't need to recall them in detail. Novel situations may carry more useful data, or new learning material.

Learning is not just about sitting in school during the formative years of your life. Learning is also about remembering faces and being able to connect them to roles, histories and predicted behaviour. We learn the personality dynamics in the office, and we learn our way around a new town. Every physical skill we master, every concept we get to grips with and every idea we take onboard is part of our learning process. Our brains never stop learning.

Sometimes learning dreams are entirely obvious. If you continue in your sleep with things you did in the day, these are probably learning dreams. That can also be the case when we revisit books and films in our sleep. I've found computer games especially invasive in this way. Entertainment is no less an experience and our minds need to figure out what we're going to do with that, and what we need to learn from it.

It's worth noting that learning dreams are not dreams about being back at school. Learning dreams connect in obvious and direct ways to things we have experienced recently, while awake. The more metaphor and symbolism there is in the dream, the more likely it is not about learning, or about sifting through recent memories to store them. It may be the case that we do some mental housekeeping around longer term memory, and that this throws up stranger imagery. However, this may be harder to spot if there's nothing in your waking life to confirm the suspicion. Sometimes our perspective of the past changes over time, or new experience casts old events in a different light. If you suspect this is what you're experiencing, then you probably are. Reflecting on the dreams and your feelings about more historical events in your life may help to clarify this. Reworking the stories of our past can be a powerful agent for personal change. The journey from the story of being a victim to the story of being a survivor, for example, allows us to reimagine ourselves. It may be that dreams will prompt you to reconsider how you view your own past, or come as a consequence of unconscious shifts in your perspective.

Day-to-day learning dreams are indicated by their clear and direct relationship with waking life. In the dream you will be doing something similar to the wakeful learning activity. It may be exaggerated, distorted, or a bit surreal, but the gist will be apparent. If recognisable details are significantly complicated by additional features that were not in the waking experience, this may be about processing your emotional responses to what has happened. New learning situations can be exciting, or they can make us feel anxious, and these responses are likely to colour our dreams.

Some learning clearly engages our body chemistry to a significant degree. The activities that could kill us if we get them wrong manifest as adrenaline and stress toxins, all of which can still be in our bodies when we later try to sleep. The chemical process of new love, or of new parents bonding with a baby, can translate into dreaming. When we engage our bodies in physical learning, we're developing muscle memory, and that goes with us when we sleep. So, waking or sleeping, we may be having exactly the same chemical responses to life, and just manifesting our understanding of that in different ways. If you aren't able to consciously think about what's happening to you – if for example it would not be okay to admit to yourself that you have fallen in love with someone inappropriately – this is even more likely to show up in dreams.

We may also use dreams to test ideas, exploring 'what if' in a way that may help us make choices when awake. If there are decisions to be made in life, consider that your dreams may be testing out options, imagining potential outcomes and offering you insights into how you might feel about all of that. Most dreams are not predictive in the sense of foretelling the future, but your dreaming mind is perfectly capable of trying to predict your responses to anticipated outcomes. This is a case of your mind chewing over what you already know. Your dreaming mind may be wiser than your waking one and therefore may make better predictions. It may equally be true that your dreaming mind is too heavily influenced by emotional possibilities to make the best judgements. Working out where and how we do our best thinking is an individual process, but one that confers considerable benefits. Knowing where our strengths lie, we may better gauge which impulses to trust.

One of the things we do when processing a dramatic experience, is decide, on some level, whether it was normal or not. People who suffer from post-traumatic stress disorder tend to learn trauma as something normal. Repeated trauma makes this more likely (war zones, domestic abuse, jobs exposing you to violence or distress), but it can happen with one-off horrors as well. Nightmares are a common symptom for PTSD sufferers, and it is worth wondering whether the process of normalising trauma creates nightmares, or whether the nightmares are a process of normalising trauma. Our dreams, or more often in this case our nightmares, can give us some sense of what we're doing with life's harder experiences. If we keep dreaming the trauma such that we normalise it, there are obvious dangers: we are internalising the idea that this is how the world works. It might be possible to work consciously on our dreaming in order to change our relationship with an experience. Methods for working with dreams will be explored later in the book. Revisiting trauma can cause more harm than good, and is not something to do lightly. Professional support may be appropriate in more extreme situations. Revisiting distress is uncomfortable, but much safer. Working with nightmare imagery might give us a safer way to try to deal with profoundly difficult things.

Often our dreams are not this tidy, but instead blend real world experience, imagination and aspects that are harder to explain. Whatever the surface of your dream suggests, it is the emotions that are the most reliable indicators of what's going on. Your dreaming mind does not need to tell complex stories to express feelings in dreams. You just feel them. However, emotions tend to be entirely internal events, which makes setting them in a 3D context a bit more difficult. It is the expression of emotion that I believe creates much of the strangeness in our dreams. Look for the relationship between the surface details and the emotional content as a starting point for any attempt at interpretation. Things that do not coherently fit together are often the most revealing.

If you treat your dreams as side effects of rational brain functioning, and explore them from that perspective, you may find an increase in their function as a rational, processing method. I have found dreams to be curiously responsive to the ways in which we consciously choose to work with them. Perhaps this should not be surprising: it is, after all, us.

Chapter Three

The Dreaming Heart

Emotions do not need to be repressed in order to colour our dreams. While our conscious, intellectual minds move quickly, our feelings are far slower creatures sometimes, while at others they move so rapidly that reason cannot keep up. Often, we respond to experiences with our intuition first, and only bring reason to bear in order to justify what we've already decided. At an emotional level, we can have a lot going on and coming in, without being fully aware of it. Dreams are a means by which we can explore and process all of that.

While more intellectual issues in our lives can be resolved by thinking, that which is essentially emotional can take a lot longer to work through. Shifting relationships and changes within ourselves can often be slow processes rather than easy to identify events. I also find that the bigger an emotional issue is, the less able I am to reason my way through it. Feelings have to be felt, and big feelings can't always be felt all in one go. They need time to mature and develop, to evolve, grow and for me to respond and change as required. Thinking about that as it happens can be productive, but only when that's even possible. Sometimes it takes a while before deep emotions bubble up to a level where we can reflect on them.

When it comes to big life changes, to healing, bonding, grieving and loving, some of the most important things we do can initially happen unconsciously. Sometimes the best thing to do is not try to wrest conscious control of the process, but give it the time and space to flow. Some things work best if allowed to ferment slowly in the darkness. Too much light and scrutiny makes for a lousy batch of wine! There is a degree of letting go called for in this, and trusting of the deeper levels of self. Our culture encourages us to be immediate, rational, in the moment, and in control of ourselves. Often what our emotional selves, our bodily, animal selves, need is the exact opposite. We need the space not to know, to be hovering between past and future, and drawn into both. We need to have our minds wandering purposelessly and to relinquish control over our feelings. Only by this means can we get to our own authentic responses and find out who we really are, what's really happening for us and see from there, what we might actually need.

Accepting that we don't know what's happening within us is difficult, and there are pressures to feel like we should be totally self-aware. When there are big life events unfolding, it can seem like we really should have a good idea of how we feel and what we want – it doesn't always work that way. Dreaming time can give us a chance to handle things less consciously, and more fluidly. Emotions are often slow, but give them time and they do work themselves through.

When our dreams are driven by our emotions, it is feeling that will colour what we experience. How we represent that to ourselves will depend on the symbols that make most sense to us. We may be very literal in our expressions. We may draw on personal experience and the resonance of iconic moments, items and people from our own lives. Equally, we might take our symbols from our culture. In the coming sections, I will be considering dreams in terms of their emotional impact and making suggestions about how to understand emotional dreams. If your dreams do not leave you with any distinct feelings, they probably aren't directly linked to your emotional life.

If you do not have clear or detailed memories of your dreams, then consider your mood on waking, and explore from there.

Darker Dreaming

Our fears, frustrations, grief and losses can all colour our dreams. These are often related to each other, feeding off each other and perpetuating each other. Pain denied and grief repressed can feed into feelings of powerlessness and hopelessness. Only when we recognise our pain and dysfunction can we make changes in our lives to alleviate our own suffering. The act of recognition alone, honouring the existence of our more troubled, less socially acceptable feelings can in itself bring some respite and break cycles of despair. There is little worse than feeling that you must appear, or (more appallingly) feel, cheerful, positive and grateful when the reality of your life makes you angry, miserable and demoralised. Being able to own negative emotions allows us to be whole people, while having to fake positivity can destroy self esteem.

Anxiety Dreams

Typical examples:

- Sitting an exam you are not prepared for.
- Being hunted or chased.
- Being in physical danger.
- Needing to do something important but there being some barrier to that.
- Being unable to move normally or at the appropriate speed.
- Being unable to control your own actions.
- Getting lost.
- Making mistakes.
- Toilet doors that will not shut.
- Accidental public nudity.
- Inappropriate behaviour, or situations of public humiliation.

Sometimes there is a direct relationship between the anxiety in the dream and the source of your waking fears. Worries about appearance can show up as hands growing out of your face. The person who feels persecuted may dream that they are being hunted. Someone who fears social humiliation may experience dreams in which they are unhappily naked. The things we fear may show up in large and obvious forms, able to chase us across car parks with tax returns in their mouths. We may replay traumatic or uncomfortable incidents, or explore things we were afraid might have happened. The near misses and the worst case scenarios can get into our dreams if we are worrying about them.

It is important to note that most dreams are not prophetic. Dreaming that the thing you fear comes to pass is not evidence that you are doomed. All it shows is that these worries are preying on your mind. Take the worry seriously because it is real and the causes need tackling. Do not let the anxiety dreams convince you that they are portents of the future, such that they feed your fear!

If fear dreams are more convoluted, and you cannot automatically connect what is clearly a fearful dream with something that is troubling you, here are some questions that might help.

- Is anything in your life threatening or unsettling you? We can be reluctant to admit fear, even to ourselves, but only when we get it out into the daylight can we deal with it.
- Is there unresolved distress in your past? There is no logic to when these things resurface, and an old wound can turn into a new nightmare.
- Are you inexplicably fearful when awake? Illness and exhaustion can do this to your body; it may simply be that you need more rest and less stress in your life.

If your answers to these questions are all negative, and you've only had one anxiety dream, then the dream is probably not that significant. If more anxiety dreams follow, you will need to reconsider those questions to try to make sense of what's happening. If you have answered yes to any of them then you need to explore the underlying issues and resolve them. If the issues are considerable, you may need professional help. Most of us experience modest levels of anxiety at some times in our life, especially around major life events. If this gets on top of you, simple interventions such as cognitive behavioural therapy can be a great help. Sometimes, a few days of rest, a few good meals and a walk can be enough to break the grip of stress and get us back where we need to be. If you continue to suffer, get help.

If you suffer persistently from anxiety dreams and cannot find any obvious explanation for this in your life, check to make sure there is nothing in your sleep environment that could be causing your problems. Being too hot or the room being too stuffy might be explanations. It may be that your situation is more complex and you may be suffering while not being consciously aware of the source. For example, some bullies can be subtle, using unobvious and psychological methods to wound their victims. If we're constantly being blamed or found fault with, we will become anxious whilst feeling that we are inadequate and to blame, rather than seeing the problem as something that is being done to us.

We can be unwilling to admit to ourselves when there is more stress in our lives than we can actually handle, fearing to be seen as weak for failing to cope. Anxiety is presented to us as an individual problem, but it is a consequence of exploitative, insecure capitalist society. We may blame ourselves for things beyond our control, or shoulder more responsibility than we can bear. The more intense and frequent anxiety dreams are, the greater your need is to identify what is causing them. If they are regular events, they have a cause. The body and the dreaming mind can be a good deal more honest about identifying that which is unbearable; it is our conscious minds that try to deny it when we are in trouble, all too often.

Fear can become a habit. If we are exposed to fearful things then over time, our bodies may decide that fear should be the default response in many, or all, situations. We can come to feel that we need to be afraid of everything. Repeating fear dreams can be a sign that we need to get our fearful, historical experiences into perspective and under control. It is a hard thing to admit and to face, especially when your body has learned fear, but it can be unlearned, and doing so is a great quality-of-life improver. If you feel that fear is your friend, that it helps you to stay safe, protects you in some way, and if fear is escalating in your life, then you may have learned fear as a bodily response. Cognitive behavioural therapy is a good tool for this one. The logic is that if you break your unwanted patterns somewhere, you can change things. Pick the easiest place to make changes – that might mean studying your thoughts for signs you are telling yourself to be afraid, and then deliberately creating new thought forms. It may mean changing your behaviour patterns so that you stop reinforcing fear. The hardest thing to directly change is the emotion itself, but recognising when it happens and looking hard at the cause helps to change the patterns.

It is always worth asking – what are you really afraid of? If there is fear in your dreams, it may well be because you are not acknowledging or dealing with fearful things when awake. Rather than denying or negating your fear, the anxiety dream can be an appeal from your dreaming mind to take the emotional response seriously. Get to grips with the causes. Know them, name them, and see what you can change or overcome in order to become more at peace in yourself.

Shame

Shame and desire can be closely related, but while desire comes from within, shame is often shaped for us, by our culture. Fears of disapproval over what we do, or want to do, accompanied by fears of ostracism or humiliation tend to underpin shame. Our bodies can often be focal points for shame, as we are encouraged by endless advertising campaigns to dislike our furry, imperfect animal selves. Several thousand years of demonising sexuality has its influence as well.

Cultural assumptions about who we 'should' be; as parents and workers, children, voters, consumers, lovers, can all lead to feelings of shame. We may be too ambitious, or not ambitious enough. We may be childless, or have too many children. Irresponsible, or anally retentive. Too original. Too sheepish. Too fixed, or too fickle. No matter how we are, and no matter how modest our desires, there will be someone around to disapprove and to judge us. Occasionally that negative feedback can be helpful; alerting us to things we might truly want to change. More often, those who wish to shame us are jealous, sadistic, or in denial about their own shortcomings. Telling which situation you are in is never easy.

If the intellectual decisions we come to about humiliating experiences, or our fear of them, are at odds with our emotional responses, dreams centred around shame are a possible conse-quence. While a sense of shame is part of what enables us to live co-operatively with other humans, the power to humiliate can be used to control and damage people. If you are being shamed by an individual, it can be hard to tell if they represent the opinions of everyone around you. Group shaming is not definite proof of personal failure, either. Deciding whether we have an issue that we need to fix, or if we are surrounded by unpleasant people and the answer is to step away, is a hard call to make, and an essential one if we are to function as responsible human beings.

For example, a person who feels shame around getting angry may have a short temper and may need to learn how to control that. They may also be in a situation where they are not allowed to be angry, and are punished for expressing reasonable anger in the face of unreasonable behaviour.

If we carry guilt over our actions (justified or not) this too can manifest as shame dreams. If we do not trust ourselves, or antic-ipate being tested and are not sure we will do well, then shame dreams can pre-empt anticipated humiliation, and may be a form of preparation for dealing with feared failures.

The shame dream itself will have a public or exposed aspect to it. While the focal point of the dream will probably reflect some aspect of the shame experience, the details can be fairly random. For example, feeling uncomfortable because professional people were scrutinising my life, might have been what prompted me to dream of a breast growing out of my face. That commonly experienced dream of being inappropriately dressed – ghastly fashion failures and exposed genitals – can all be manifestations of body shame, sexual shame and fear of public humiliation.

Shame is not an experience many people are willing to own or discuss. The nature of it means we do not want to draw attention to it, which makes it hard to explore whether our shame is well founded, or unfairly forced upon us. If we can establish that the attempt to shame us was unfair and unjustified, it is a good deal easier to recover from the experience of humiliation. Righteous anger becomes an option. However, the faintest suspicion that we have reason to feel ashamed is profoundly uncomfortable. It calls into question our most basic qualities as people, and can, in challenging our actions, bring the validity of our personalities and beliefs into question. No one goes there gladly. Either we resist with aggression (if only verbal) and attack the source of the accusation, or we try to bury the feelings. Alternatively, we may have no self esteem, and may internalise the faintest hint of criticism, becoming burdened by a weight of shame. The tension between what we desire and what we think, or know will be acceptable, is the source of shame. The less able we are to deal with that tension, the more likely we are to dream about it.

The uncomfortable likelihood is that if you are experiencing shame dreams, then on some level you do think you are in the wrong. That which we have accepted and dealt with does not tend to come back and haunt us. The only way forward is to draw the issues out into the light and look at them properly. Face what you've done. If you have trouble working out how bad it is, consider how you would feel if someone else did it. Would it be a forgivable error if a friend did it? Would it be okay if someone treated you that way? Try to build a bigger context of what is acceptable in order to look at it in a more balanced way. It may be that you are harsh on yourself, or letting cultural pressures feed your shame over innocently human shortcomings.

However, if your actions have harmed someone, or something, or your desires would if you manifested them, then your shame is a prompt to act. The only route to peace is to start changing yourself, to become someone you can like and respect. If some aspect of your behaviour is toxic to others, you have to change what you do. There is nothing else. There are no easy answers if your dreams are showing you the things you do not like about yourself. The responsibility lies squarely on your shoulders. If you have been capable of feeling shame over your shortcomings, then you are also capable of fixing them.

Lost Things

Dreams can take us into the past, either as it was or reinvented by our current emotions. History is a tricksy thing – memory is subjective, understanding changes over time, recollections distort. How we feel now colours how we understand our history – when depressed we are more likely to recall unhappy times. If we only dream about things from our past occasionally, it may be nothing more than tidying up our long term memory. The time to pay attention to the history dreams is if you keep revisiting something. Either the past is being used to try to express something of the present, or there are unresolved issues. Also be particularly alert to revisiting things that are no longer in your life, that have changed so dramatically that the original is no longer available, or that are being radically re-envisaged in your dreams. When we've moved on easily and naturally from some aspect of our past, it will not tend to trouble our sleep.

Sometimes, revisiting lost things is nothing more than grief over the absence of something that was once dear to us. This acknowledgement of loss and absence is perfectly natural. If you know what you are missing, and the dreams are nostalgic or mournful in a way that makes sense to you, then these dreams are exactly what they appear to be and require no further interpretation.

It is when your dreaming mind obsesses about the past in ways your waking mind cannot easily explain that you need to go deeper. What is the emotional association with the time, place, person or object you keep going back to? Are you craving the security or lack of responsibility that you had in childhood? Is it the bliss of ignorance that you miss? Do you long for the energy, wellbeing and ambitions of your youth? Was there a time when it all made more sense, was happier, or more functional in some way? Is it about feeling safe, or about a time when you had more hope and belief? What might you have lost within yourself that is reflected in these dreams of lost things? Have you lost something external without recognising its true value to you?

Dreams of lost things can direct you to places of insufficiency in your life. We can become tied into the responsibilities of our adult roles such that we forget the needs of heart and soul. We stop having time for the things that used to make us happy and that used to give us a sense of identity. Sometimes, our hopes and aspirations die, or we give up on them. Life is not as we imagined it would be, and we forget something of who we used to be and what we once aspired to. Plans for revolution are replaced by a desire for a new kitchen. It is so easily done.

The lost things dream is very likely a cry from your heart to go back to the things that used to matter to you. The things that you have become too grown-up and busy for; the important things that slipped through your fingers while you were running after a career and all the status symbols. If you dream of lost things, you have not forgotten who you are or what matters to you. It is time to open the door and let some of that back in, or to find new ways of expressing heart and soul in your waking life.

Grief

There are aspects of grieving that are very physical. Left to run its natural course, grief can take us through rage, denial, calm, and weeping in cycles until we are able to reconcile ourselves to the loss and make peace with it.

We tend to underestimate the power of grief when it does not involve a death. Loss of job, home, friendship, country, hopes, beliefs, status, health and so forth can create deep wounds that take time to heal. All significant losses can lead to grieving. The less time we give our waking selves to adjust to the loss, the longer it tends to take to actually reconcile ourselves to it and move on.

Part of the reconciliation process involves unpicking all the things we thought would happen and removing those from how we had been picturing the future. The aborted aspirations are less visible to those around us than more obvious losses, but are no less painful. We do not always know what we've built up around a place, a person, a job, until that is no longer available to us. How we see ourselves, where we think our lives are going, how we derive meaning from our days can all be tied to external things, and if we lose something that was key to who and how we were, it can take a lot of adapting to. We need to re-imagine ourselves and our lives without that which is lost to us. Faced with a devastating loss, it can be hard to imagine how life is to continue. Building that sense of how on earth we go forward is an important part of the recovery process.

That which was not conscious in the first place can be much harder to deal with when lost, than something we knew we needed and valued. How do we begin to mourn for something we weren't aware even mattered to us? Even recognising the loss can be difficult. Some of the things we depend on, we may not even like having to recognise. The tension of a difficult relationship might be key to our ambitions and drive. Someone else might be carrying aspects of our lives in ways we don't want to acknowledge. We might have addictions, co-dependency issues, obsessions, habits. We might be hooked on things that are toxic to us, and in letting them go, be unable to process the grief of loss simply because we don't want to admit there is a hurt. We can take for granted the things that sustain us, failing to notice what has always been dependably there.

Working through this kind of complex emotional difficulty may be something we tackle with our dreaming minds. While this may run close alongside what we do when we dream of lost things, any denied and therefore unexpressed or unconscious grief may lead to more convoluted dream expressions. This will take some unpicking and is not easy to interpret. There are also usually reasons that we took for granted or underestimated things now lost to us, and those reasons may still be active alongside our grief. If there is incomprehensible grief in our dreaming, we may be experiencing this. If you are crying in dreams, if there are significant absences – literal holes in your dreaming world, if you're always looking for something and do not know what, or are yourself lost and unable to find or remember important things, this may be a sign that you are grieving and have lost something significant without consciously recognising it.

Normal grief runs as a process through our minds and bodies. If we do not let that happen when our loss is raw and immediate, it can be much harder to deal with. Delayed grief is a recognised issue, and as this is a hard thing to deal with, proper counselling may be required. If, years on from a loss, we are still suffering from grief dreams, there may be issues to address. Are we unable to let go? Do we want to let go? Sometimes we need to carry our losses with us, they are too big and too important to set aside, despite social pressure to get over it and move on. Are we carrying guilt? Are there regrets around things we did or did not do? If there are unresolved issues around the loss, that can make it harder to process our grief.

Unexpressed pain, unvoiced anger and unanswered questions can haunt the living long after the dead have moved on. The grief of loss can be less of an issue than the grief of problems unresolved. The dead cannot explain, or apologise.

It falls to the living to make peace with the past. Dreams inspired by grief are an invitation to own whatever pain you carry. Although we are too often told otherwise, it is okay to speak ill of the dead. Some of the dead were total bastards when alive. It is fine to be angry, to resent their going, to rage over what was not said and to be furious about the things we got wrong and can now never hope to fix. It is fine to grieve over things that were better way back when, and the aspects of self we were required to bury in order to survive. Grieve for your childhood sorrows, and the shocks of growing up. Grieve the lost dreams and abandoned hopes. Grieve the life that was not lived, the paths not walked, the opportunities that never came, the wrecks, ruins, mistakes and disasters. Name it, own it, and claim it. Only then can you make peace with it.

Death

It can be alarming to dream of death; be it our own or someone else's. Death in dreams can function in a number of ways, but because the nature of this experience will tend to frighten us, and colour the experience, it isn't always easy to work out what we're trying to tell ourselves.

Dreaming of death can be a simple expression of reasonable fear. Experiences that make us conscious of our own mortality can have us dreaming about death just as a way of processing the information. Fear of death is a good thing insofar as it helps us stay alive and manage risks sensibly. If the fear of death paralysis us such that we also become afraid to live, we are in trouble and should seek help.

Life changes routinely kill off parts of the self. The child in us 'dies' to make way for the adult. Loss of aspiration and hope can kill off bits of us. It is all too easy to build an identity around what we imagine we will one day be. Recognising that hasn't happened is a moment of personal death. Equally, we can kill off the fears and assumptions that have held us back, finding freedom in the death of bits of self that were doing us no good at all. Death is not always a bad thing. There must be death in order for there to be life. If the old does not fall away there is no room for the new to flourish in our lives.

Death in dreams can therefore reflect periods of transformation, or suggest the need for radical change. If this interpretation makes sense to your waking mind, then engage with it, and find out what is dying for you. Take that journey consciously because it is much more effective if you do.

In spiritual terms, death can be an important part of the journey. Shamanic practitioners will talk about more and less literal death experiences as forms of initiation. Sometimes it is necessary to die to your old life and be eaten by spirits before you can carry on with your work. We might think of Odin on the world tree, Ishtar in the realms of the dead, or Gwion dying to Ceridwen to be reborn as Taliesin. Christians talk of being born again – which certainly implies a death, while Buddhists talk of the death of ego as a spiritual goal. Many spiritual paths will call upon you to die to an old way of being in order to embrace something more soulful. Death in dreams can therefore be an expression of your spiritual journey, or a call to nurture the spiritual side of your life.

When we dream that someone else has died, a number of things can be happening. It might reflect a change in our relationship with them. A part of them might have 'died' – the friend who settled down when you didn't, the sibling who moved away, the guy who was injured and had to leave the team – death can simply represent dramatic change. We may also use people to personify aspects of self, projecting characteristics onto them, or fears, or hopes. Thus the death of someone in a dream may be a projection of some inner process.

Unless you have reason to be sure you dream prophetically, it is safer and wiser to assume that dreams of death are not portents of actual, bodily death for you or anyone else. Most usually, dreaming about dying has nothing to do with physical death. There is also a myth that to die in dreams will kill you. It won't, and the threat of death in dreams is nothing to fear. I have lost count of how many times I have died in dreams and I have not died bodily on any of those occasions! Sometimes the experience is disorientating and unsettling, but that is the worst that can be said of it. In dreaming, death is nothing to fear.

Rage

Anger is the least socially acceptable emotion. Often, we are measured as reasonable, rational adults precisely by the degree to which we can control our anger. Curiously, in certain contexts though, rage is accepted as a justification for domestic violence, verbal aggression, assaults, and even murder. We find atrocities explained by extreme emotion to be more acceptable than violence undertaken calmly and for a more considered reason.

Whether we are allowed to get angry or obliged to be docile says a great deal about our status. Oppressive situations are quick to take away our right to get angry, because that paves the way for all future infringements to go unchallenged. Girls in many cultures have traditionally been raised to be 'nice' and not therefore, to argue or object. Learning to accept all things passively is not good for us. The person who is not permitted to get angry is vulnerable to being abused. Rage is an important tool for self-protection.

However, useful though rage is, when it is thwarted, it can readily be turned inwards. Some theories suggest that this internalised rage leads to depressive illness.

Not all rage is good for us. The rage of a person who must preserve their self image at any cost, is a toxic thing. The rage of challenged tyranny can be brutal. Prejudice and intolerance, when called out, will rage to defend their right to hate. We can use rage to intimidate, to destroy difference and to crush dissent. Where rage implies violence (and it often does), even the hint of it can be enough to muzzle all protest. Violent and aggressive language use is threatening enough, without a subtext of physical danger. This too can be used to create fear, and in fear, obedience. This abhorrent behaviour is sadly all too common.

Rage in dreams will most likely manifest as some form of violence or destruction. Dramatic natural violence – volcanoes, earthquakes etc – may serve as good symbols. Rage will come to us in dreams where it causes problems for us in waking life. If we are furious but unable to express rage, and are also healthy enough not to subvert that into self-hatred, rage in dreams may be clear and manifest fairly literally. Perhaps we will punch down buildings or blow up symbols of our frustration.

If we live in an oppressive situation, we might not even be able to be honest about our anger with ourselves, it being more bearable to pretend everything is fine. Rage dreams may be our wiser, dreaming self trying to alert us to the danger we are in and to prompt us to act. Many victims of abuse are persuaded that they are to blame for their experiences and so become unable to manifest healthy anger. If your dream self is enraged, you need to work out what, in waking life, you ought to be getting angry about. If you realise you are living in a dangerous situation, seek police advice and be careful – more people are seriously injured or killed when they try to escape from abuse than at any other time.

What happens if yours is the rage of the tyrant or the frightened ego? How do you tell if your rage dream is a product of oppression or a consequence of your being an oppressor?

Many perpetrators express feelings of being in fact the victim, and this story helps them to continue harming others, without feeling any guilt. How do you tell if you are the problem? I think the answer has everything to do with fear.

Over-defensive egos that must be right at any cost are full of fear. Tyrants are afraid of those who might take their power. Would a tyrant dream the pure fire of needful rage, or would their dreams be twisted by terrors of being treated the way they treat others? I suspect the latter. To understand your anger, look closely at your fear. This tells you what you are trying to protect or compensate for with your rage. Ask what of your own behaviour you would find tolerable in someone else. Are you afraid of being seen as wrong, or afraid of getting things wrong?

There is a world of difference between wanting justice, and wanting revenge. There is just as much difference between wanting your own power, and wanting to have power over others. How you dream about rage may tell you some vitally important things about yourself. If you are capable of facing up to an issue in yourself, you are also entirely capable of changing. However, those who are sadistic to the core may not even doubt themselves in dreams. Those who strive to do the right things for the right reasons may be less willing to trust their own motives, and a little doubt about ourselves is a good thing. None of us are perfect; all of us make mistakes and have blind spots and weaknesses. Very few of us are wholly good or entirely evil.

Nightmares and Catharsis

Experiences change the structures of our minds and bodies alike. We can turn genes on and off by mechanisms we barely understand, while memory may be held in more than just the brain. Fear, trauma, pain and deprivation, along with all lesser degrees of suffering, impact on us in very physical ways.

It has long been known that trauma causes nightmares. Certainly since the horrors of the First World War there has been some awareness that hideous experiences in life will translate into nightmares. Devastating experiences take some grappling with, so it is little wonder that we may enlist sleep to help us in that process.

I think that one of two things can be happening when we experience nightmares. The first option is that, in our nightmares, we are learning the trauma. We are processing it into a new understanding of how the world works, which will embed the trauma and leave us with open wounds to the psyche. Where people suffer one-off horrors, this is less likely. However, for those who come out of war zones or abusive homes, there has been much more scope for normalising trauma. Nightmares can become normal if normal life has become a nightmare. If in our waking lives we find ourselves obliged to try to cope with ongoing distress, our nightmares may be our only clue that what we're trying to render normal in order to cope, may not be something we should be complicit in.

If all, or a significant number, of your dreams are nightmares, look harder at your waking life. There may be some very real problems you need to address. If you are trying to persuade yourself that things are okay really, or that they are bound to get better if only... it may well be that you need to stop doing that and start acting to protect yourself.

Either as a parallel process to this or as a second way of understanding what's happening, nightmares may function as a cathartic outlet. This is especially likely if the trauma is clearly behind us and we feel secure, or are actively engaged in a healing process. Nightmares can also be a process of unlearning the trauma and de-normalising it. This can be a re-processing, re-interpreting experience that allows us to re-invent our memories and think about them differently. We may be considering that what happened to us was not inevitable, reasonable, normal or deserved. This is a huge process to go through, so it affecting our dreams, or partially happening through them, seems likely. The process of recovering from trauma can be distressing in its own right.

If the prompts of your nightmares cause you to re-assess your circumstances such that you realise you are in danger, be very careful. Do not challenge your aggressor outright, and avoid anything that may escalate your problems. Seek help and plan a safe and careful escape. If the situation is grim but not this dire – a domineering boss, an unfair relative – again avoid direct confrontation as that will likely only inflame things, and see what you can do to improve your circumstances. Sometimes, just knowing that your treatment is unjust makes it easier to bear without also losing your self-esteem.

If you are having nightmares as a consequence of historical distress, consider seeking professional help. It can be really useful having someone to support you through the recovery process. One of the great advantages in speaking to a professional is knowing that you are not responsible for protecting their emotional wellbeing. They have been trained to listen to terrible things, and knowing this can make it much easier to air what was otherwise unspeakable. If you prefer to handle this alone, be aware that re-visiting traumatic memories tends to make things worse for most people. You do not need to dwell on memories of your trauma in order to heal. Focus on rebuilding your sense of what should be normal, and what you should be able to expect, and keep your attention on moving forwards gently.

We all have nightmares now and then. If they turn up occasionally with no particular patterns in terms of content and no obvious triggers in your life, they probably aren't too significant. Trapped wind causing discomfort, a cramp in the night or some other minor physical consideration may be to blame. A nightmare that taps into memory might suggest we've had and repressed terrible experiences can be deeply disturbing, but if it is a one-off, might not mean much. We can repress trauma, we can also end up with conditions that give us delusions, and it is a good idea not to leap to conclusions when faced with something that suggests one or the other possibility.

If you get a lot of nightmares but no discernible patterns of content or waking-world correlations, take it as a cue to be kinder to yourself. Try to take some time off, get more rest, pamper yourself a bit by whatever is your preferred method. Slow down, move gently, and see if this changes things. Your worst case scenario is that you get to be nicer to you for a while.

Up-Beat Dreaming

Not all emotionally inspired dreams are born of pain and anxiety. If we have rich, reasonably happy and more fulfilling lives and are largely free from inner conflict, we will likely have a much more positive experience of dreaming.

Most of us are not wholly happy creatures or endlessly miserable ones. We move between the good times and the bad, with a broad spectrum of experiences and responses available to us. Dreams can give us some measure of how we are doing, and for the person who is less emotionally aware in waking life, this can be especially useful feedback. Knowing that there is a value in signs of happiness, watching for those signs and nurturing that which enables us to be happy, changes things. We engage in a positive feedback loop, making more space in our lives for the good stuff.

Quality of life is not about being a cog in the corporate machine, or a never-satisfied consumer. Finding what gives us genuine joy and discovering what enriches and inspires us is important. Once we have that knowledge, we can work with it, to develop more space for the good stuff. Not only are we rewarded in our waking lives, but our dream life becomes happier and richer, too. This does not lead to some magical New Age state of perpetual joy. Life will knock us down sometimes. However, the person who knows their own needs and priorities, knows how to seek their bliss and is able to notice when life isn't delivering that, will overall be happier.

Perhaps the most insidious destroyer of happiness is banality. That life might be sufficient in terms of material comfort, busy enough to keep us running around, and has enough people in it to feel engaged – yet fails to deliver something. We can have a lot of fairly superficial experiences but not feel the depth of emotional engagement or mental stimulation we actually need. A great many casual acquaintances may be no substitute for profound friendships. Many people come to Paganism because they seek a deeper and more meaningful experience of life but need that to be grounded in observable reality. There is no single right answer to how we achieve this, but watching where your dreams go, and how they reflect your days can help you spot the things that are working for you. If certain people, places, or activities tend to inspire richer dreaming, you know where to invest more time and energy.

Ironically, obvious thrills and excitement – that which gives us an adrenaline hit – can often fail to deliver an antidote to banality. Like many consumable drugs, adrenaline is something we can develop a tolerance to, needing ever more extreme things to provoke a response. Drugs and alcohol only work because they tap into our existing body chemistry, and all parts of our body chemistry systems are vulnerable to overload and burnout. Those who seek rapture in pornography can find that same issue of tolerance and the need for ever more extreme hits. Visual violence might give us a 'hit' but this too can pale, and if we aren't careful, these acts of sensation seeking can leave us feeling more lost and empty than ever. Those on a religious path can find they have to get ever more extreme in their practice in order to feel what they need to feel, too. It's this, I suspect, that has extreme devotees torturing their bodies in search of enlightenment. Starving is popular, but there are many ways to mortify the flesh and many religious traditions that will cheer you along as you beat yourself up in search of the divine.

I don't have any answers to this, only the experience to say that ultimately, extreme practices tend to lead to crashes, not anything we can live with. Anything can become banal, with repetition. The only thing that seems to work is to instead cultivate a love of the small things. There is a great array of 'small things' out there – so much diversity to love, and thus far at least, I have not burned out or become mired in banality by doing that. I do not promise that it is a dependable solution.

The process of transferring information between waking and sleeping can create cycles and feedback loops. Nightmares are themselves disturbing and depressing. Bad dreams can colour our waking hours while a good dream can set you up with a cheerful mood for the day. Our emotions colour our perceptions and that shapes our experiences. Dreams can, by this means, have some very real effects on our waking life. A cycle of gloom, night-mares and feeling disturbed by the nightmares can lead to seeing the worst in everything, holding more gloom and spiralling down. Equally, cheerful dreams that uplift us may help us make the best of a day, see the funny side, find the positive bits and so come through exactly the same set of experiences feeling reasonably upbeat. These are cycles that can quietly perpetuate themselves without ever being noticed. These circular, self-reinforcing experiences can be broken into at any point and we can change how we experience the world when it hangs largely on how we interpret it.

Happy Dreams

Warm, cheerful, affirming and unthreatening dreams frequently do not require a lot of analysis. These dreams feel good because they are good. Most likely they are a reflection of a healthy and untroubled body and mind at rest in a good space. If you get one of these, or many, enjoy them for what they are and do not worry about poking around in the symbolism for deeper meanings.

Happiness does not have to have deeper meanings and is largely possible because we know how to enjoy things as they are and in the moment. If the dream suggests things that make you happy but which you'd not been giving much time to, that's well worth taking note of. If your happy dreams suggest directions you might take in life – 'an' it harm none, do what you will!' Knowing what makes you happy is an important piece of self-knowledge, and the person who knows what gives them joy is better able to live a rewarding life.

If you are getting weird and convoluted happy dreams, this has interesting implications. If the appearance of the dream is complex and bewildering, or seems at odds with the cheerful emotions, it suggests that happiness is not a straightforward issue in your waking life. Perhaps you feel guilt over things you enjoy. There can be many reasons for this. Enjoying too much cake isn't good for us. Many of our happy vices have consequences that are less happy if we overdo it. We may feel guilt because we are happy when others are not, or we are aware of being privileged while so many others in the world are deprived. Perhaps there are people around us who resent our being happy. On a more sinister note, we may find our joy in things that involve too much greed, cruelty, or selfishness to be acceptable.

There are all kinds of reasons why we might not want to recognise the implications of happiness. Owning when we are happy might, by association, force us to admit where we are not. Be that at home, at work, in our families, our culture; the implications of being happy some other place can be life changing. Perhaps we aren't ready to make the leap into a whole other life, even if joy calls us to do that. Perhaps we have duties and obligations that prevent us from honourably taking the plunge.

We can't always manifest our feelings nor do what we most want to do. However, we can hold a private, inner space for ourselves in which we know, name and honour our true desires – whatever those are. We can do that in order to know ourselves.

Holding that knowledge, we will better spot the opportunities to move closer to that which we desire.

If our true desires are appalling in some way (an attraction to children, a delight in causing non-consensual pain) and we undertake to know that, we can also try to control it. Unconscious suppression is not a great strategy. If we know our desires – be they ever so deviant, we can find ways to work with them. The skills that make a great torturer are not far removed from the skills that make a great surgeon. Psychopaths can be very capable politicians and business people. Murderous inclinations make for great works of fiction. Dentistry would be unviable as a profession without a ready supply of people who can cope with professionally inflicting pain. Being happy in yourself has a lot to do with finding ways to work productively with your own nature, be it ever so flawed and peculiar.

Desire

Sexual desire in dreams can be nothing more than an expression of bodily need. This tends to have an impersonal quality, but can be confusing if we borrow someone we know and are not normally attracted to in order to express it! Dreaming that you desire someone, does not mean that there is necessarily any kind of unexplored attraction there. It might be about qualities that person embodies for us, or be because they were on our mind for some other reason and that collided with our hormones. If you desire someone in a dream but do not desire them in waking life, or have no interest in pursuing them, treat the dream as interesting information, and carry on as usual.

If we feel ashamed of our lust or find it inappropriate, then lust in dreams can manifest in ways we find especially uncomfortable on waking. Dreaming of sexual activity we would not normally wish to engage in can be deeply disconcerting, which can feed into and reinforce underpinning feelings of shame and guilt. Consider how you feel about your own sex drive and how your culture or background has taught you to feel about it. Being able to accept that we simply have mammalian bodies with sexual appetites can go a long way to easing the discomfort. Recognising that not all of us conform to perceived norms around desire is also important. Some of us are not innately sexual beings, and that's fine too.

The more at ease with our sexual identities we are, the better chance we have of either not being troubled by unwanted sexual dreams, or of getting ones that are enjoyable.

Our dreaming, emotional selves can be more aware of slow growing attractions than our wakeful, rational selves are. This is especially true when we aren't looking for emotional involvement; when other factors seem to preclude it or we are not naturally alert to our own emotional responses. Inexperience around desire would be a consideration here, too, as the less experience of attraction we have, the harder it can be to spot the early stages. Thus sometimes, to dream that you are attracted to someone may be a very realistic first sign of romantic attraction, but not a guarantee of it. You may also have picked up some body language or vocal cues that suggest said person is attracted to you. We filter out more information than we are consciously aware of, but sometimes details we've not considered will surface in dreams.

We measure our capacity to love and desire by our experiences to date. For the person who has really only felt mild enthusiasm before, and not known there might be more to attraction than this, the realities of unbridled lust and passionate love can be a shock to the system. The sudden shift in perspective about everything that went before is disconcerting enough all by itself. If you think you know what it means to love, and then get the emotional equivalent of being hit by a truck, it can be hard to fit this into your understanding of your own feelings. The conflicts arising from this can show up in dreams as we try to process the unfamiliar responses. To imagine you know, and then to find out that you had no idea whatsoever, is a startling, if not shocking process.

The desire we feel in dreams may be less about the other person and more about our own needs and feelings. We may want to feel loved, or to be found attractive. We may be craving affection, attention or security and have sent ourselves a message about this based on sex. What we understand sexual contact to mean will likely inform what we're saying to ourselves when we dream about it. If we find sex affirming and see in it evidence that we are loved and desired, then sexual dreams express this to us – perhaps as forms of self love, or as reflections of need. If sex is shameful to us, then sexual dreams can really be shame dreams. If we are not at peace with our own urges and desires, the conflict between mind and body can inform our dreaming.

A bad-sex dream may actually be a fear dream. If we have anxieties around emotional vulnerability or nudity, that might be expressed by dreaming of a sexual scenario. If we've had bad sexual experiences and sex is in any way fearful or threatening, or has been used to control us at some time, our dreams around this aspect of life may be troubled. Dreaming about it can help us work this through, providing safer spaces in which to explore, and safer material to reflect on as we try to heal.

If sex is a good and positive feature of our lives, we may use sex dreams as a way of expressing that we are feeling good, confident, desirable and so forth. For some people, sex and power are strongly connected so that dreams of sex may be an expression of how powerful, or powerless, you are feeling.

The chemical process of emotional bonding is largely the same across all kinds of relationships. Consequently if you are in a process of bonding with someone in a profound but non-sexual way, you may get sex dreams as a side effect of your body chemistry. That can be very misleading as it may suggest sexual attraction where none exists. I would suggest not taking too seriously any sexual dreams that turn up early on in making a connection with someone, especially if that kind of interaction seems weird when you are awake. Such dreams may be experiments in working out how you feel, but they are not predictions nor are they reliable reflections of your own desire. That said, if dreaming about sex with someone causes you to realise that you really are attracted to them – that's worth considering properly.

Love

Love can be part of the experience of desire, or wholly separate from it. Love in our dreams may be a simple reflection of the love we feel when awake. This is not likely to stand out as unusual. It is more likely to be loves and passions that we aren't exploring that come back to haunt our dreams noticeably. Old flames, relationships that never were, places we never went or haven't been back to – where there is longing we may be more likely to dream about love. The desire for love or a sense of its absence can inspire us to dream about it. We can also use dreams to practise, testing out our feelings and responses before we commit to anything in the waking world.

For those who believe in reality and deity as full of love towards us, dreams might be a space in which we express that to ourselves. It is worth considering the direction of flow in dreams – does love flow from us, towards us, or both? It is easier to experience love in the form of our own feelings when awake, but the sense of being loved can translate into dream material. Feelings of warmth, security, affirmation and acceptance may be associated with feelings of love. Of course our feeling loved is not always a good measure of whether we are loved.

Holding a sense of the world as benevolent and loving does seem to work for some people, while others have to go to considerable, uncomfortable lengths to uphold the belief that everything is ultimately lovely. There is often a relationship between feelings of being loved by the universe, and privilege. If you are affluent, healthy, educated and otherwise comfortable, the world is bound to feel like a kinder place than it does for someone who is poor, ill and struggling. If we see this as love rather than luck, it can take us in some less compassionate directions when it comes to thinking about those less fortunate than we are. I get very tired of New Age writing that claims the world and the divine are pure love, because clearly for far too many people, that's a brutal and abusive kind of love at best. I don't have a lot of time for the kind of 'love' that will beat a person to a bloody pulp and tell them it is for their own good. The idea that this universe is a bit neutral and mostly couldn't care less about me or anyone else, leaves me a lot more comfortable than the idea that this is what love made manifest looks like. That may be why I do not dream about love all that often.

Quest and Journey Dreams

Quest and journey dreams are distinctly different from the dreams of lost things. Rather than hankering after what was, the questing dream sets you in pursuit of some new thing. You may know what it is – a destination to reach, object to find, person to seek out or an achievement of some sort. You might not know, but be striving after it anyway, with a sense of purpose carrying you forward. There's a forward looking quality to the quest dream.

While lost things dreams tend to be mournful, anxious or nostalgic in tone, quest dreams are innately hopeful. They leave you feeling inclined to get out there and do something. The only difficulty may well be in figuring out what it is that you need to be doing. There may be elements of the dream that suggest a sense of the direction we already want to take in waking life. If nothing obvious strikes you, then just spend time with the idea of the quest and the journey. Ask where you are going in life and what you want. If there's something unconscious wanting to be manifested, then waking or sleeping, sooner or later you will start to determine what you want and how to move towards it. When the hankering for change is upon us, it tends not to take that long to find some way of moving with that desire.

If you have reached a calm and settled point in your life, the quest dream can suggest a desire for excitement and new challenges. There may be nothing calling you forwards, and no already existing desire to unearth that will reveal the path to you. It might instead be that you are just bored, dissatisfied, craving change, adventure or inspiration. This can often be the case with midlife crises experiences. The desire for novelty, excitement or meaning can be pressing, but with no obvious signs as to where we might go. While we might find inspiration in dreams, it comes down to us as individuals to create our own meanings and directions. Sometimes, desire needs nurturing and developing, especially if we've spent much of our lives putting other people's needs ahead of our own. Sometimes what we have to quest after in the first place is our own desire and only when we create the want and let it flourish within us can we tell how to move on, and get on with doing something about it.

If you are fermenting ideas or gestating projects, the quest dreams can be a simple side effect of all the planning. At this point, the quest dream may have more in common with learning and fettling dreams designed to sort out memory and figure out life. The dream itself may not give you any great revelations about what you're doing, but means that your waking mind is really on the task and that you are invested in the process. Absence of questing dreams at the start of a project is not something to worry about – it may be that your conscious mind has it all in hand and no further consideration is required.

Sometimes we set our ambitions aside to attend to practical things, or because we put other people's needs first. Sometimes we wait, gathering whatever tools and skills are needed for the leap into the (almost) unknown, and the shift from preparation to action can be challenging. At other times, fear and doubt will hold us back from jumping when we know we need to. Perhaps it wasn't the right time, before, and we waited for the moment to come when we could do something we longed to attempt. Perhaps we were not ready, but now start to feel as though we are, and so the quest dream calls us to step up.

If we dream of quests and journeys, and if our sleeping lives are more driven and adventurous than our wakeful ones, we may be ready to take a big step forward. We may need to get out there and live a bit more, take some risks, and give ourselves opportunities to fly.

Rapture and the Numinous

There are dreams that take us far beyond normal experience and into something so laden with wonder and so rich with magical feelings that a deeper significance is implied. Any dreams that inspire us to want to bring something of their glory into the world – as songs, stories, paintings or other actions – fall into this category. These are the dreams that touch our souls so we feel blessed, more whole and more capable when we wake from them. These are the dreams of rapture.

The numinous is not readily pinned down in words, but is at the heart of all spiritual experience. A sense of the numinous can elevate the most mundane things, allowing us a glimpse of the magical within the familiar. We catch sight of that which might be divine, sublime or insane. This is an experience that can be found in dreaming and in waking life alike.

A person deeply engaged in their own spiritual work may find numinous dreams to be a natural, affirming and glorious extension of their waking devotions. However, sometimes the numinous simply comes to us, unsought, so that the blessing is devoid of context and sense. An impression of profound meaning, arriving with no explanation, can tease at your mind and isn't always comfortable. It seems to demand something from you but may never specify what, exactly, is being asked for. Visions of gods with clearly phrased requests are not how these experiences always tend to go outside films and ancient, sacred texts. Some dreams can feel incredibly numinous even while having no elements that this seems attached to. Simply, some kind of light, or rich and fertile darkness, permeates the dream; shining through it. There may be no symbols to work with, no messages to uncover. The numinous just is, and declines to explain itself. There is no reason to assume that the numinous has conscious intent. Deity may have conscious intent, but the numinous is not perfectly equitable with the divine.

We may have a sense of the numinous when working with deity, and imagining it or experiencing something of the divine. An experience of the divine is likely to be inherently numinous, but the reverse is not true – the numinous is not inherently divine. A person with no belief at all can have an experience that is spiritually uplifting, gives a sense of connection or inspiration such that it is a numinous moment for them. No sense of deity is required. I suspect that anyone with a firm belief in deity will understand the numinous on those terms, while people with less certain belief will use other points of reference to make sense of things as best they can.

How we experience wonder and symbolise the sublime will vary between individuals and depends a lot on our beliefs and culture. We tend to mediate such experiences through familiar symbols. That goes far beyond religious icons, and can relate to any aspect of our lives. Sometimes, god is a DJ. If we do not have a belief system to help us make sense of experiences, then that which brings us ecstasy or resonates most deeply with our waking selves will give us a means to express the numinous in dreams. Powerful emotional experiences, beauty and inspiration all have scope to convey a sense of the numinous to us, or express it for us.

There are a great many ways that the numinous can manifest in dreams. Our own sense of wonder is the most important indicator. Freedom from the usual restrains of physics and biology – flying, breathing under water, travelling between stars, through time, at great speed or over great distances may be examples of numinous dream experience. We may see the life in all things, or the connections between things, or gain a sense of mystical truth that we cannot always carry back to the waking world.

Numinous dreaming is not inherently prophetic. The forms we use to express wonder to ourselves may just be convenient, and not literal. If gods speak to us in dreams, for example, we can respect that experience without assuming it to be a literal truth. However you feel about deity, any experience you have is filtered through your limited, human mind and any actions you take are solely your responsibility. We need to apply wisdom, compassion and common sense to our choices of action, even when our dreams appear to be demanding the extraordinary.

Where numinous dreams differ from all other kinds is that they do often suggest to us some kind of external agency. Numinous dreams often leave the distinct feeling of having been touched by something other than our own imagination. Engaging with that possibility raises a great many questions about how we think reality works and what we imagine dreams to be. Such experiences may be better understood in spiritual terms rather than by attempting to rationalise them.

One point I would encourage you to take from such experiences, is this: any wonder or sense of spiritual bounty we are capable of feeling in dreams is also available to us when we are awake. We might clothe the experience in dream symbolism, in the language of flight or of wild fancy, but those feelings of awe and wonder belong to us, and whatever we make of the cause, the experience itself is real and valid.

A numinous dream can either cause or reflect great shifts of awareness within us. We become more open to possibility and inspiration and, as we open ourselves to that, more numinous experiences can come to us. There's often a very fine line between awe and awful, but the more able we are to accept and to flow with such experiences, the less alarming they become. We can be inspired, waking or sleeping, without being entirely overwhelmed.

It is the numinous dreams that seem to demand most explanation while at the same time often denying any hope of rationalisation. Our rational, waking minds desire to have everything make sense. The numinous dream often suggests its own significance while refusing to clarify what we are to do with it. When something feels that important it is almost inevitable that we demand to know what it means and therefore, how we are supposed to respond and act to carry this significant moment forward in our lives. However, the numinous dream is a gift, not an instruction. You do not necessarily need to dissect it nor is it always essential to understand it. Simply accepting and letting it affect you can be a good deal more beneficial than trying to unravel a single, clear meaning.

Getting to Know Your Dreams

Before you dive into any attempts at deep analysis of meanings, it is worth getting to know your dreams. Find out about these differences between bodily informed dreams, emotional dreaming and learning dreams. Get to know yourself as a dreamer and develop an overview of your dreaming life. This will give you a context in which you can consider any specific dream. You will have habits. Some things will be normal for you, others unusual and more noteworthy. Understanding the broad themes and trends in your dreaming will also make it easier to get an overall perspective of your life. The better able you are to see how your dreams relate to your life, the easier it is to spot the things that might be important.

Dreams are a lot better at telling you where you are and where you've been than they are at predicting the future. They reflect recent experience, learning, memory sorting and emotional concerns, and are often intertwined in what we do when awake. That feedback on waking life can be really helpful for seeing where we are, cultivating self honesty and looking after ourselves. Learning to read the present is a worthwhile activity. It is from the present that the future will be born, and the choices we make today inform the options we have tomorrow. Working with the immediate, with the patterns of life and dreaming, and with the way history has carried us to this point is the most reliable way of getting some control over the future. Prediction tends to be about big issues and dramatic events, but most of life is made up of the small, day–to-day details. Get those right and the bigger things more often fall into place anyway.

Many forms of divination are underpinned by the idea that something random will somehow be attuned to fate and therefore will connect with the flows of the universe and give us useful insight. When you consider the mechanics of divination, it's a rather odd process. The random card I pick from a pile will supposedly relate to what I should do tomorrow. However, irrational though it seems, it can be an effective way of working.

I've worked with divination for many years, and I think we tend to misjudge where the actual magic occurs. The cards do not know anything, and the many flows of possibility about tomorrow do not sweep by at my request to pick the relevant card out for me, to tell me what to do for the best. Instead, it is my ability to find relevance or insight in random things that tends to be useful. The most important magic is what happens in my mind; in the leaps of connection and insight and often quite random things can spark that. The important bit is the way our wiser, unconscious minds can be triggered into recognition by the introduction of some random element. What we knew, but had not realised we knew, is drawn to the surface by the turn of an oracle card or the spread of the tarot.

If you are thinking about a divinatory aspect to dreams, it is worth pondering whether you see that as the universe speaking to you directly about important matters, or as portents drawn from the chaos, or as your own wisdom speaking. If you tend to see your dreams as random, then this second option may make more sense to you. This is why it's important to spend time getting to know your dreaming habits before you start reading too much into them. If your dreams are largely informed by your viewing habits, but you treat them as a random oracle, you could end up with some decidedly strange feedback loops.

In the coming sections we'll be looking at ways to develop your relationship with your dreams.

Chapter Four

Working with Dreams

Courting Good Dreams

There are a great many very simple things a person can work on to improve the quality of their sleep, and dreaming. Many of these have been touched on previously, but are worth exploring in more detail, not just as explanations for dreams, but as points at which we can take action to improve our lives.

A dark, quiet and comfortable sleeping space is essential. Mattresses and pillows flatten over time, and as this is a gradual process we can easily fail to notice how the bed itself is undermining good sleep. Comfortable bedding and being warm enough are also really important. Your bed should be a comfortable, welcoming and happy place to be. Anything that interferes with that needs changing.

Do not take work into your bedroom or use it for stimulating forms of entertainment if you want it to also be a good sleeping space. We build associations between spaces and activities by repeated use, so where we work becomes a work space. If we repeatedly take unhappy things into a place it becomes an unhappy place, and so forth. If you are regularly anxious in a place, then you'll probably feel a bit anxious any time you go there. Your sleep environment needs to be strongly associated with rest, relaxation and sleep. There's a secondary issue in that using screens exposes us to light in ways that do not help us to settle.

So, what can you do in bed aside from sleeping? Rest, read, meditate, listen to music, massage, any kind of social curling up is good and so is lovemaking. Take phone calls from people you adore and who make you happy, but take stressful calls somewhere else. As far as possible, turn the phone off, don't check the internet. Leave as much of the rest of the world at the door as you possibly can. Hold your bedroom as quiet, private, personal space, only available on invitation. Once in this space, do not let yourself be widely available. You might want or need to be available to other members of your household, and you might well be entirely at ease with the free flow of their coming and going. However, if you need space, it is perfectly okay to discourage children, dogs, even partners from banging in and out nosily whenever the fancy takes them. Basic rules around care and respect can be brought into play here.

Allow yourself wind-down time before going to bed as this makes it easier to settle and improves sleep quality. If you are running flat out – physically or mentally – and then jump into bed, you won't settle and sleep easily. Give yourself time to do gentler things for an hour or so before bed, when possible. Wind down. Relax. This will improve your quality of life and reduce your stress levels as well as the beneficial impact it has on your sleeping.

A properly cared for body enables good dreams. Diet and exercise are important components of this, too. Ideally you don't want to eat much in the hour or two before bed. Sleep on a full stomach can have an odd influence on dreams – it's not just cheese that can catch you out this way! It's better not to be lying down to do your digesting, if possible, and there is research to indicate that carbs eaten last thing are more likely to lead to weight gain than they would at other times.

If your diet is poor; not nutritious enough, not providing enough energy, or pumping you full of too much, this will all affect your sleeping. Good food is part of your dreamwork. A tight budget can make this difficult, but anything you can do to take care of yourself is worth adding to the mix even if you can't achieve the diet you consider optimal. Caffeine and sugar both act as stimulants and are best avoided for some hours before sleep. Alcohol will also affect you and again when you are working with dreams, it is as well to stay away from the recreational substances – at least until you're confident about what you're doing and how dreams and substances might therefore interact with each other.

Deal with stressful issues and worries as best you can when they arise. Make time in which you can at least be honest with yourself about anything bothering you, even if you can't act on that honesty. Problems you try to ignore will come back to trouble you while you are sleeping. Anything you are suppressing or trying to deny will do the same. Even if you can't solve your problems, self-honesty will help you to do the best you can with what you've got. Be alert also to any signs that you are fixating on problems or obsessing over things that make you anxious. Our moods can be shaped by our thoughts and we can talk ourselves into feeling far worse than we need to.

Avoid obsessing over bad dreams. The more attention you pay to dreams, the more you feed them. Dealing with underlying issues indicated by dreams will help tackle the troublesome ones. Obsessing but doing nothing will make the bad dreams worse, or more frequent. You are simply reinforcing the problem if you dwell on it. Try to focus on real world solutions, if the nightmares are about things you can fix. If the nightmare has no obvious relationship to your waking life, let it go. Deliberate forgetting is a useful skill sometimes.

Try to arrange not to have to leap out of bed immediately upon waking. A few minutes to remember and reflect reinforces your dreaming and allows you to pay more attention to it. Having that slightly gentler start to the day is also a great comfort improver. It allows time to gather thoughts, and settle into the day, rather than setting you up to run like a hamster on a wheel, legs paddling frantically but going nowhere.

If you are regularly woken from dreams by your alarm clock then you aren't getting enough sleep. If you are getting enough sleep, you'll tend to wake naturally at the right time. Sufficiency of sleep is of great importance. If we don't get enough sleep, we may not get opportunity to dream, we reduce the healing and learning benefits of sleep, too. We have a culture that does not value sleep, and making the time for it in the face of pressures to be busy and active, is hard. However, the person who is properly rested can get a lot more done and will make better choices. Sleep is a really important investment, and if you struggle to wake up, you need more.

Some of us suffer from insomnia some of the time, or a lot of it. This is not always easily explained or solved. Sometimes our best efforts at a healthy life do not result in good sleeping. I want to make clear that with the best will in the world, we can't always get this stuff right and sometimes the body and/or mind refuse to co-operate. If you struggle with sleep and with good dreaming, this is not something to feel too responsible for. If you've tried everything and it isn't working, be kind to yourself about the problems you are having. Not everything can be fixed by working hard at it. The best thing you can give yourself in this context is gentleness and patience.

Questions to Ask of Your Dreams

Beyond considering the broad dream types already described, you can learn more about your dreaming self by asking questions about your dreams and seeing what your answers suggest. As our dream material tends to be drawn from our lives, experiences and feelings, the conscious answers we come up with are going to be of interest. In consciously answering dream questions of course we run the risk of replying with what we wish for, or fear may be true, so the process is sometimes only as useful as your level of self honesty will allow. That said, identifying what you wish for or fear may be true is well worth your time and effort – that self knowledge will stand you in good stead, and is relevant for considering any dream material in context. The essential thing to remember here is that dreams or interpretations based on our fears and wishes do not give any of that a reality outside our own minds.

You can ask yourself anything at all about a dream in order to explore it. The following set of possible questions is by no means exhaustive, but will give you a place to start from.

Are You in Control?

Are you able to think and act freely in the dream or do you experience it passively? Are you able to think about what's happening but unable to choose what you do? Is your self-control only partial? For example, you may find you can react, but not at a normal pace. If this is the case to any degree, consider why it might be happening. Is this a meaningless one-off or a reflection from your waking life? How in control do you generally feel, and are you comfortable with that? How do you feel about what's happening in the dream – how does the loss of control affect you emotionally? Is it frustrating, unsettling, or a bit of a relief?

If you have normal levels of autonomy in your dreams, how does that impact on how you experience the dream? Do you normally feel in control of yourself, or is this unusual? Do you want to be in control, or would you prefer the feeling of being swept way?

Do you have control over other aspects of the dream? Are you able to create it or direct it in a way normal reality does not permit? How does that connect to how you feel about what's happening? Do you want to be in control of everything, or does that sound like a hideous amount of pressure? Do you feel safer when in control and, if so, what are you safe from?

The degrees of control, or the lack of control, you have while dreaming can tell you about your current relationship with power and authority, and how able to self-determine you feel. Whether you have control in your dreams may reveal things about your fears and cravings. Do you want control over others? Do you like feeling unable to choose what happens to you and thus not having to feel responsible for the outcomes? Are you apparently powerless in dreams and doing things you would not otherwise feel it is acceptable to do?

The dream is also you, and everything happening in it is also your choice, regardless of whether or not it seems like that at the time. When we dream we're powerless, we can be giving ourselves permission to act out things we do not really believe we're allowed to do. Giving ourselves unusual power can be a reflection of how powerful and great we feel, or it might reflect being asked to take unreasonable amounts of responsibility.

In our waking lives, we negotiate through constantly changing levels of influence and control. We can be important in some contexts and a bit part in others. Some aspects of our lives are determined by other people, government dictate, or blind chance. If we take too much responsibility for things we have no control over, that can really demoralise us. If we fail to recognise luck and opportunity in our experiences, we can get very distorted ideas about our worth and capability. In waking life we need to be very alert to issues of power and responsibility, and as these are almost constantly shifting, they are issues we may need to dream about in order to figure them out.

We may well be learning and processing issues of power and control at an unconscious level. Identifying that process consciously gives us the option of looking at what is happening in this aspect of our lives, and making more deliberate choices about how to handle that. People can all too easily become cultured into acquiescence. Slow erosions of rights and dignity can be surprisingly hard to spot. Life pressures can shape our behaviour in ways we don't notice. It may take a dream inter-vention to flag up that something is going steadily wrong – especially if it's in an area of our lives where we don't want to admit there's a problem. Whether we turn out to be the overbearing partner, the pushy person, the downtrodden worker, the tyrannical boss... I think it's better to be aware of the power roles we have adopted in our waking lives so that we can consider whether we want to be that person.

Who Are You?

In your dreams, are you your normal, waking self? Do some parts of your identity and personality manifest more strongly than others? Are you harking back to a former self, or imagining the person you hope to be? Are you taking on roles and characters like an actor in a film?

How much of your dreaming identity depends on the situation you find yourself in? Are you a distinct character, or malleable, changeable and shaped by the context?

Are there dreams when you are not yourself at all? Do you go so far from your waking character as to be unrecognisable to yourself? Do you become another person? A different gender? Another species? Are you locked into one identity, or comfortably settled in it? Are you lost and trying to find yourself, or empathising your way through many forms? Is your identity creative and explorative, or limiting?

How do you feel about the person, people or others you become when you are dreaming? What does that tell you about your feelings towards yourself? Are there aspects of yourself that you wish to express, but normally feel unable to? Are there things within you that you find troubling?

We are innately playful and creative creatures, so dreaming we are other than ourselves can be entirely about having some fun. It can be a way of exploring empathy and different perspectives, or can let us experiment with our options a bit. If it's an experience that you feel comfortable with and happy about, you can assume it falls into that category. If there's something uneasy about perspective shifting, it may need more attention. If you repeatedly dream you are someone else, then you need to look at the relationship between your dream identity and your waking self to figure out what's going on there.

Again, exploring these questions is all about self knowledge. Dreams can and will show us the things we try to hide from our conscious selves. The shadow self we would prefer not to exist at all. The lost child. The person we set out to be. The person we think everyone else wants us to be. The roles we have that we can't live up to and the roles we wanted. Many of the buried pieces of self are buried for reasons – they are not convenient in waking life. They do not fit in with the demands being made upon us or the realities of day-to-day living. They are not viable, not likeable enough, not wanted. Burying does not make them go away, and we can haunt ourselves in dreams. Those ghost selves, those denied parts, can have gifts to give as well as challenges to offer. We are richer if we get to know them.

How Are Your Senses Working?

Not everyone manifests the same set of senses dreaming as they have when awake. Some people do not dream in colour. Some dreams lack sound. Tactile information may be missing. Can you taste things? Do you have a sense of smell? Do your senses all work normally in your dream? Do you have senses while dreaming that are not normally available to you? It's interesting to ask if there is any relationship between our dreaming senses and our waking priorities.

The old myth about pinching yourself in a dream to see if you wake up depends on the idea that we do not feel pain normally in dreams. My own experience has been that I can feel considerable pain in dreams. I've also died, while popular theory has it that this is not possible, and that you must either wake up before the moment of death, or actually die. In dreams, all things are possible. We can feel things that are not available to us when awake. I have bodily sensations when dreaming that I can't articulate because they have no relationship with any waking experience I am aware of. This has happened to me for years and I have no idea what, if anything, it signifies.

How do sensory experiences in dreams relate to your waking, sensual life? Are you sensually aware, or do only certain kinds of information filter through into your awareness? How do your dreaming senses relate to the emotional content of the dream and, by extension, to your emotional life? If you have extra senses not normally available to you? If so, what role do they serve? Do they reflect demands you are otherwise unable to answer? Do these extra senses cheer or trouble you? Would you want these senses when awake?

Our dream senses may give us insight into how we feel about our actual, bodily senses. Dream senses can also suggest needs, desires and problems we are struggling to manage. If we're expected to be psychic by bosses or partners, we may give ourselves psychic powers when dreaming. Areas in which our waking lives are under-stimulating may also become apparent. If we don't have much tactile contact when awake, we may not bother with skin sensations at all while dreaming, or we may over compensate.

Coherent or Confusing?

Do your dreams usually make narrative, or emotional sense? On waking, can you describe what happened in the dream, or is it so incoherent that it cannot be put into words? Are your dreams a reflection of linear time and normal reality, or are they made of chaos, where none of the regular rules of physics or causality seem to apply? Do you tend to get a mix of regular reality and insanity? If there are shifts between the two, look at when and why this happens, as it might tell you something.

Dreams that make some degree of narrative sense are easier to talk about, to rationalise and to analyse for possible meanings. The more incoherent a dream is, the harder it is to extract features that could be made to mean something. Are these just white noises from the sleeping brain, or do they have their own kind of significance? Is the chaos itself potentially informative? What effect does it have on you if you get a dream that defies description? Are you comfortable with that, or do you find it unsettling?

It may be the case that chaotic dreams are indeed nothing more than white noise. I observe them in myself during periods of light sleep, especially first thing in the morning. They often seem to make sense for the few seconds while they occur, but all logic disintegrates, or proves to be absent, when I try to think about them afterwards. I am inclined to dismiss the vast majority of brief, incoherent dreams as just things the mind does.

However, incoherence may also feature in dreams when we are trying to grapple with ideas that are otherwise unthinkable for us. These might be concepts that we do not have words for, desires we do not yet know how to name much less sate, fears too vague to have formed definite shapes yet. Rather than being small irrelevancies, it may be the biggest issues of life and self that we are struggling to make sense of. All cultures and languages limit our scope for expression in various ways. All have topics that are not easily expressed or that we're not encouraged to explore. We only have one word for love, and our individualistic language makes it harder to talk about collective experience and community. There are feelings we should not have and urges we are meant to deny and we are to hide our hungry, flatulent animal selves under a veneer of civilisation. The harder it is to even acknowledge something exists, the greater our chances that, on encountering it, we will have incoherent dreams.

It may well be that, in time, the unthinkable will slowly evolve into something you can express to yourself. If your dreams are largely incoherent, then patience and compassion towards the less acceptable sides of yourself may be needed to help you resolve that chaos into something that makes more sense.

Is There Uncanny Knowing?

Dreams often have a logic of their own. The rules of the dream reality may be self-evident as we encounter them or utterly bemusing. It is interesting to ask how it is that we become aware of the truths and rules in our dreaming worlds. As we have (most usually) invented all of these things, it is obvious that we should know, which makes it more interesting when we don't have that insight. Sometimes dreams come with details about the history of the setup, its future, and the feelings, motivations and intentions of various participants. This process raises some very interesting questions.

How we tell ourselves the rules can be revealing. Do we find out by trial and error? Are we told by a dream character we've endowed with insight? Do we simply know without needing it explained? How far does our knowing extend? Do we limit ourselves so that we only know the kinds of things we'd be aware of if this was a waking situation? Do we know we are dreaming? Are we being honest with ourselves that this is something we've made and that therefore the rules are entirely our own?

How much insight do you think you have when awake? How does that compare with the insight you imagine you should have, and how much you think everyone else knows? How does that compare with how you experience dreams? Do dreams reflect your experience, or are they more like representations of what you think you should magically know? Conversely, are you uncannily under-informed in dreams? If we made the dream, how much of it are we hiding from ourselves? Do you lack the insight any person could expect to have when awake? How well informed do you feel and how does that play out in dreaming?

Knowledge is power. To be denied knowledge is to be vulnerable. To be expected to know things that you have no way of knowing, is alarming. Having too much information can be distressing. Do you want to know more, or less? If a deity offered you an apple in a dream, and you knew perfectly well which symbolic apple it was, would you accept, or decline?

Uncanny knowledge in dreams can tell us how honest we are being with ourselves. If we often know we are dreaming, and if we often have a sense of what's going on, what the story is, how the dream works and so forth, this suggests we are in the habit of being honest with ourselves. If we are in the habit of lying to ourselves, that can carry through into dreams, to be expressed by our having no idea what's going on, or why. We may not even understand our own actions.

There are a great many reasons why a person may not be honest with themselves. It can be all about protecting fragile egos, or giving ourselves a license to act out. It can be about refusal to grow and change. We can also lie to ourselves when we're in harmful situations, so that we do not have to feel badly about the person or circumstance hurting us. If the job we love won't pay the bills, or our child takes us for granted, we may lie to ourselves to make that more bearable. Self-delusion can have the most honourable motives. Sometimes it can be decidedly helpful as a coping mechanism, where truth might be unbearable. It is not a black and white issue.

For Pagans, there is the additional issue of the pressure we may feel to experience something uncanny or supernatural. Much of this will depend on who you interact with socially and how they talk about uncanny experience. If you feel expected to have supernatural experiences, but don't, this may colour your dreams. Plenty of Pagans will talk about hearing the songs of spirit and getting requests from deities, but when really pushed for details about that, often back down into more modest claims about inspiration and poetry rather than any kind of literal truth. As there's a fine line between spiritual experience and madness at the best of times, the pressure to experience life in slightly insane ways can be a truly uncomfortable one. It is not a competition. You are not a failure as a Pagan if trees don't talk to you and you've never seen a deity. Work with what you have.

Magical or Mundane?

Are your dreams akin to more mundane life experiences, or do they give you something else entirely? I believe that if your dreams are shaped by the books, films, games or other entertainment in your life, that you can understand that as a reflection of your waking experiences, too. If these have more impact on your dreaming life than, say, your day job, it tells you something about your preferences, and perhaps your desire for escape. Where we find emotional meaning, joy or the answer to other needs will have a reality for us, and that needs taking seriously.

Your dreaming mind may not be able to distinguish between a waking day at school and one lovingly imagined at Hogwarts. We process entertainment information just as we have to digest all other forms of input, so dreams reflecting that side of our lives are still dreams about life. The imaginative life is no less 'life' in terms of how our minds handle it when asleep. I think that says some very interesting things about how we are as people, and how we view existence. We tend to treat the playful and imaginative as some kind of optional extra – frivolous and not so important. Yet, for some of us, the 'make-believe' parts of life are the most affecting and rewarding. As a culture we invest vast amounts of time and money in escapism, but that only appears to be acceptable if we do it while reminding ourselves that it is trivial and silly. That could stand a rethink.

It is when we engage imaginatively with life that we are able to innovate. There is no creation, no change, no new technology or new stories without this playfulness. Every made object around you was imagined into existence. What starts as make-believe goes on to shape our actions. The more open we are to possibility, the more we can do in this way. Without speculative thinking, all rational thinking can do is dissect what it already knows.

If in dreams you invent places you have never been, people you've never met and experiences you've not had, it is a good deal harder to explain what's going on. Where are you getting the raw material for this dream from, and why? Are you dredging up forgotten memory, or creating something entirely new? Why are you creating this? What is it for? How does the experience of it affect you? Are these dreams invigorating, or exhausting, or do they have little impact?

The less obviously explicable a dream is, the more tempting it becomes to dig about in it for possible hidden meanings. Often there are no definite answers to why we dream of certain things. However, the bigger picture may reveal something. The trend in your dreams towards the magical or the mundane may reveal something of how you feel about your life. That in turn will be influenced by how you feel about the magical and the mundane in the first place. If you are a creative person in any aspect of your life, then those creative muscles will flex when you are sleeping, and that can produce all kinds of strange and colourful results.

Is the dream an act of escapism? Are you comfortably rooted in the meaningful realities of your life? Do you crave adventure or novelty? Do you feel trapped in a predictable waking existence? Are you regretting the life choices you made? Do you feel some insufficiency in yourself? Are you world-weary and craving the simple comforts of hearth and home? Does your waking life leave no time for creativity and imagination? Are you afraid of thinking about other possibilities?

Ask what it is that you want, and where it is that you feel most comfortable. What are you drawn to, and what are you seeking? What does the balance between the magical and the mundane in your dreaming tell you about the balance of your waking life?

Narrow Dreaming

Are your dreams diverse, or restricted to a few basic narratives with identical, or very similar shapes and content? Do you always seem to be doing the same sorts of things, or do you always wind up in the same places? If your dreams are very narrow in their content, is this because your life or your future prospects also seem very narrow to you? Are you fixating on one area of your life at the expense of all others? Are you denied, or denying yourself, opportunities for growth, change and adventure?

We make stories out of our lives, and we make lives out of our stories. Sometimes we can get so caught up in a role or a story that we do not give ourselves a chance to be anything else. Sometimes we can be stripped of our freedom in situations that seem to demand we behave as though everything is fine, when it isn't. Bullying partners, or employers, or a health problem to cite a few common examples, may make us feel we have to close down our options by pretending everything is much better than it really is. Maintaining the old story – that we are strong, on top of things, healthy, equal to anything – may be more important to us than dealing with things as they really are. Sooner or later, that becomes impossible to maintain, and the consequences of that can be tough indeed.

There can be many reasons for narrow dreaming; a narrow life, narrow expectations, undernourished creativity, loss of hope, lack of scope for self expression and others. Whatever the reason for it, having a narrow array of dreams is never a good sign. Something is wrong in your life. Some part of yourself, your prospects or your experiences is not as it could be, or not as you want it to be. The precise nature of the problem may not be revealed by the content of your dreams. It may be that you feel the lack but have not identified the problem, even unconsciously. Sometimes the most telling aspect of narrow dreaming lies in the absences. What is missing from your dreams? How does that relate to your waking life? When did things change for you?

Narrow dreams, because they are innately dull are not that self announcing. It may be necessary to experience a lot of them before you register their existence. The problem is only going to become visible if you notice that over a period of weeks, and if you care enough to notice. The narrow life can make narrow dreaming hard to spot. All too often the important message held by narrow dreams is dismissed. They do not demand attention in the way a nightmare will. If you are a narrow dreamer you may also be reluctant to confront the problem anyway – that can be a big part of why your dreams are narrow in the first place! This is an easy problem to let yourself overlook, but there will be something real and significant underpinning the dreams. There may be no drama in the problem, but that doesn't prevent it from eroding your identity and life. Sooner or later, you will need to deal with it.

Repeated Dreams

Revisiting the same content in dreams is usually significant. Be it a plot, setting or participants, to keep dreaming about the same things suggests something is on your mind that needs dealing with. If the repeated dreams are banal, or reflect your waking life very closely, it may be that they are better treated as narrow dreams, instead. What we're looking for in repeated dreams is a fixation on certain features of the dream – something less about dull repetition and more suggestive of obsession or a nagging issue that won't go away.

I have commented repeatedly that dreams can reflect our learning process. That isn't always smooth and simple. Learning to ride a bike may give you a few nights of cycling dreams but unless you really struggle, or get into extreme cycling, that should be it. However, learning your way around the complexities of social interactions – on joining a new company for example – takes longer. If things in our waking life confuse us, we can struggle to work out what we need to be learning in the first place. If we are getting conflicting messages we might find that difficult to resolve. Which message are we to learn, and internalise? Other conflicts will give us difficulties too. When we dream, our minds can be trying to find more creative ways around apparently intractable problems.

Repeating content in dreams may well indicate that you are struggling with an issue. It may be that a little reflection makes this obvious, even if solutions are not forthcoming. Consciously recognising a problem can take it out of dream thinking and into deliberate thinking, and this can be an advantage.

Sometimes, when our circumstances seem hopeless or impossible, we collude with the problem by going into denial about the problem, or by ignoring it rather than naming it. By quietly refusing to acknowledge the issue, we deny ourselves any scope for doing something about it. Perhaps we are ashamed to admit our confusion, or our possible shortcomings. Sometimes, recognising that we've been put in an impossible situation has implications that we do not know how to bear. Perhaps we have to face up to some uneasy things about our lack of long term thinking, errors of judgement, or questionable motives. It may be that someone else has put us there, through need, greed, selfishness, desperation, error, assumption, vindictiveness... we may not even know why. We may be afraid to find out what those motives are, or to question the other person's intentions. Co-operation may feel safer than challenge. We may feel duty-bound to respond to demands. We may not want to consider that someone we love or respect means us ill, or is using us.

It is also the case around issues of health, money, family and status, which we can try to convince ourselves all is well in the hopes this will magically make it so. We don't get the lump checked out because if we don't know it is cancer... perhaps it won't be cancer. We don't open the unpayable bills or deal with the solicitor's email. Perhaps we even manage to banish these problems from our conscious thoughts. They will come back to haunt our dreams, though, while the practical problems remain unsolved. Challenges that we don't step up to tend not to vanish when ignored. Often what they do when festering in the darkness of our dismissal, is get bigger. The bill attracts interest, the lump doubles in size. Facing up to things is usually better, and at least then you're dealing with a defined problem, and not all the things it could be.

There is usually a real-world issue shaping repetitive dreams. They are a symptom of a fixation – either something we're obsessing over, or obsessively denying. It is therefore likely you will find some correlation between the content of the dream, and the problem. It is also likely that once you start considering such dreams, the issues will be obvious to you. In essence, you are talking to yourself about something you know you need to deal with. Turn that into conscious contemplation and the dreams should stop repeating themselves, especially if you take steps to resolve your issues.

Are There Dreams?

Are you dreaming reliably? When did you last dream? If our sleep is too brief, or too shallow, we will not dream properly. A poor diet can unbalance brain chemistry and this will also disrupt our dreaming. Mostly we do dream even if we don't remember it. Often, when people say that they do not dream, what they mean is that they do not remember dreaming – and this is not necessarily the same thing. There are qualitative differences between not remembering, and not experiencing.

Long patches of not remembering dreams have the same implications as narrow dreaming. It suggests mental and emotional exhaustion, a severe loss of creativity, it may go with depression as well as lack of time or quality in your sleep.

If you usually wake feeling refreshed and in a decent mood, then not remembering your dreams does not matter very much. You probably did dream, but it either wasn't coherent or inter-esting enough to stay with you. If you wake in a disturbed emotional state and do not feel rested, and do not remember dreaming, this is more troubling. Such experiences suggest more physical sleeping problems, or an inability to hear the things you are trying to say to yourself. Conscious work is required. Start by looking at your sleeping environment and the amount of time you devote to sleep – as these are the easiest explanations and most readily tackled. If that does not answer the absence of dreams, try giving yourself more time on waking to see if you can catch at least some sense of having dreamed. Make it your deliberate intention last thing before you go to sleep that you will remember your dreaming – you won't get an instant result in all probability, but it can help over time.

If you do not dream but are also not suffering particularly, then the answer is probably to give yourself more time and opportunity. Before you sleep, think about dreams you would like to have. On waking, try to have a few minutes when you can stay in bed, able to hang on to any fragments you can remember. Often it is less a case of not having dreams, more a case of not having the time to remember them. If we do not recall dreams on waking, they will slip away from us and we lose them entirely. Paying attention to dream recollections as we surface helps to bring them back, and the habit of paying attention will help us become more able to recall our dreaming.

If none of this resolves your issues and you are either having dreams and not recalling them, but feeling the impact, or apparently failing to dream, look at doing more work around courting good dreams. Put more into your life that nourishes you emotionally and feeds your imagination. You may be short of suitable material to work with.

The loss of dreams is a loss of opportunity for adventure, inspiration, self awareness, catharsis and more. We are better off when we know at least a part of what we dream. The loss of dreams is a loss that needs taking seriously, because it tends to be a symptom of wider life issues, and because you are deprived of something precious when you are unable to recall dreams.

Is it Good Dreaming?

Are you having good dreams? To dream well is to have a broad range of dreams that are not generally distressing. Having some darker material is a perfectly reasonable part of the mix. These dreams will normally reflect aspects of your waking life, facets of your emotional life and let your imagination run free. Good dreams are enriching and either uplifting or cathartic. Such dreaming improves the quality of our lives.

If your dreams make emotional sense to you, then whatever is happening in your life, you probably have it in hand. It's a good indicator that you are dealing with, managing and coping with any challenges that you have, also that you feel comfortable about your life and are satisfied by it.

If you aren't at that stage in your dreaming, but are instead getting a lot of banal, unsettling, distressing, incomprehensible or otherwise unwanted dream content, there is work to do while awake. If your dreams are not as enjoyable as you wish them to be, you need to identify and resolve whatever is causing that. Interpreting your dreams may be a useful tool to help you in this process. However, it is important to remember that dream interpretation is simply a way of exploring ideas that might help you to act effectively. Dream interpretation is not a solution, nor is it an end goal in its own right. If you treat it as a game, it will not lead you to anything especially useful.

Obsessing over difficult dreams and their interpretation is not conducive to good dreaming or to a good life. Not all dreams are innately that meaningful, just as not all waking experiences are life-altering. It is worth recalling Ovid's idea of the gates of horn and ivory. True dreams emerge from one gate, mere phantasms from the other. Even to the ancient Romans who took the idea of dream deities seriously, it was apparent that not all dreams had to mean something.

Often, good dreaming is something you can enjoy for its own sake, without needing to read in some kind of magical, mystical element. To assume that magical meanings are present in all dreams is to devalue the precious few where that might really be the case.

I have seen it written on a number of occasions now that most of us, most of the time, have bad dreams rather than good ones. It's a sobering thought, but if you consider the state of the world and the kinds of fragmented, unrewarding, stressful lives so many of us are obliged to lead... perhaps it is little wonder. It would take a very different culture, with very different attitudes to rest, relationship and quality of life, to result in dreams generally being good things for most people most of the time. That would be a revolution well worth having.

Chapter Five

Interpreting Your Dream Symbolism

The first question to ask, when trying to make sense of a dream, is why are you trying to make sense of it? What are you looking for when you set out to interpret this dream? If considering the emotional impact of the dream is not enough to clarify its relationship with your life and self, what makes you think this dream has a special meaning that needs pulling out? Why aren't you happy accepting it at face value? What about it seems to demand more attention? These answers should show you what you need to focus on within the dream, and which elements are actually important to you. Some aspect of the dream must have suggested a symbolic importance. Only you can judge this – it is your mind, your dream, your feelings, and your symbolism under consideration here.

When you dream, your mind is probably talking to itself. Aspects of you that cannot normally make their presence known may take this opportunity to break through into your awareness. It can be the wisdom and insight of your unconscious self that shows up. It can be the voice of your fear, or your lost inner child, or one of countless other facets of self. Your civilised waking mind may not have much time for the irrational, emotional urges of your animal self. However, those seeking peace and inner balance do well to listen to the inner voices that are not at peace. We do not achieve real peace by silencing our fears, crushing our creative urges or trying to ignore that which is disruptive and antisocial within our personalities.

Most of the time it is fair to assume that you are simply talking to yourself when you dream. The symbols you use in your dreams should therefore make sense to you, or be available to you if you give them a little thought. Unless you have a really complex and convoluted mind, complex and convoluted inter-pretations will not normally be needed. Trust yourself and trust your insight because it is your answers that matter here, and no one else knows your mind as well as you do. If you have to go to someone else, or to a dream dictionary, to get a symbol 'trans-lated' then it isn't your symbolism. At this point, the information returning to you may or may not be useful. Perhaps, like the random selection of an oracle card, it will give you an idea that sparks insight, because there is something you are aching to tell yourself. Perhaps it won't.

Interpretation is usually an act of taming. It is a way of taking the wild, uncanny, unsettling qualities of dreams and getting control of them by making them fit into a system of meaning. The standard dream dictionary is the ultimate expression of this; tidying the rich chaos into sterile one-answer-fits-all solutions. If we mean to have a wilder and more innately Pagan relationship with our dreams, we need to let go of this desire to control by imposing meaning, and be more open to accepting dreaming in its own right. This is not to wholly invalidate interpretation as a process, but to sound a very loud note of caution. It is easy to impose meaning onto dreams, and to pick meanings that suit us, fulfil our expectations and let us stay exactly where we are. Be alert to the danger that you could use interpretation to reinforce your beliefs, and avoid challenges.

If you are inclined to treat dream analysis as a process akin to code breaking, this can seriously reduce the usefulness of your dreams to you. Attaching a meaning, we may feel that we have it all figured out and can safely forget about it and move on. It is a mistake to think that interpretation means the job is done. The best and wisest interpretation imaginable is of no use to us if we treat that as an end goal and do nothing with it. There is far more benefit to be gained from an understanding that moves us forward to make changes, than there is in chalking up a symbolic meaning. Understanding a dream is a process of letting the things it speaks of truly enter your consciousness – be that ever so awkward. We can choose to open ourselves into insight rather than locking everything down with rigid interpretations of meanings we have no intention of acting on.

Why be Symbolic?

Some dreams are entirely literal. The man with a full bladder dreams of urinating. Stacking shelves for hours can lead to dreams of stacking shelves. There is no rule that says our dreams must be complex metaphors and hieroglyphs disguising greater truths.

It may be that we use symbolism as a short cut. Rather than going into laborious detail about how a series of comments at work left you feeling sexually vulnerable, the dream may give you a red cape and a basket full of food. Rather than dwelling on the ins and outs of your social anxiety around a new job, the dream may have you show up at work dressed like a 1970s fashion victim. Such short cuts direct you to a waking experience, a feeling or a moment in ways that do not take much figuring out. These symbols make sense to us, like a red on a traffic light or a toxic warning label on a bottle of bleach. We know what these 'short cut' symbols mean and can trust ourselves to recognise them.

Not all feelings are tidy and easy to explain. We use symbols and metaphors around things we find it hard to articulate. Just consider how we talk about death when awake: *At rest. Passed over. Pushing up daisies. Left this mortal coil.* The circumspect habits of our waking minds can show up in dreams as we coyly try to face up to things we generally find it hard to think about or express. Some experiences are very hard to put into words. We do not, for example, have a word or much of a concept for appreciating the sorrow inherent in the ephemeral nature of beautiful things. I gather Japanese does have that word. How do we talk about love that is neither familial nor sexual but is still powerful enough to leave you gasping? We sometimes resort to symbols because there is nothing else to use, just as in waking life, English speakers often have to turn to metaphors to talk about anything emotional. In a dream we will not say, 'This moment of falling in love was like being hit by a train.' We just get hit by the train.

Sometimes we are in denial and the tension between what we know and what we want to believe shows up in our dreams in circumspect ways. We can't entirely get rid of the unwanted feeling, we aren't prepared to face up to it and so it shows up in more obscure ways, manifesting in symbols. For example, we know we're getting walked over. We don't want to deal with the consequences of admitting we have a problem with someone. Our dreams are mysteriously dominated by carpets.

Magical Meanings

To search for a magical, prophetic meaning to dreams means accepting the idea that some dreams come from somewhere else. To our ancient Pagan ancestors, dreams could easily be messages from the gods, the ancestors or the spirit world. To the modern rationalist, dreams are all about brain chemistry, the random firing of synapses, consciousness and the interaction between personal psychology and social context. As modern Pagans we can look to both our ancient ancestors and our modern thinkers for inspiration. We can hold a middle ground where perhaps both are possible and nothing is entirely ruled out.

However, much as we might crave wonder and an experience of the divine, there are reasons to be cautious about reading messages from the gods into our dreams. I mentioned before that the numinous can be present in dreams, and doesn't always make rational sense. You can have a numinous dream that conveys no sense of deity, but a deity inspired dream absolutely must also be a numinous dream. Anything that fails to fill you with a sense of awe and wonder cannot possibly be divine.

Why should we assume that divine messages would be so

bound up in layers of symbolism as to make no immediate sense to us? This is something to be wary about. Understanding the divine as something complex and difficult to make sense of, is a concept that gives us formal priesthoods, religious authority and all the problems those institutions create. The need to interpret the divine where it isn't obviously present can put a constructed religious experience problematically at odds with rational experience and personal spirituality. The desire to see spiritual meaning can have us inventing explanations that are all about pacifying our own egos or soothing our own fears.

Even if we postulate that some dreams are inherently magical and come from another place, or level of being, clearly some of them are not like this. Some are the dreams of full bladders and tedious jobs. The desire to see magic can actually make it harder for us to experience the truly magical. If we read it in where it doesn't exist, we aren't working towards being more open, more available, or more spiritually minded. Instead, we're bigging up the small things, feeding a sense of self importance, and perhaps not even looking for the real thing. Thus we fail to grow, fail to discriminate the meaningful from the banal, and opportunities pass us by.

Over my life I have been blessed with a very small number of dreams that suggested magical possibility and perhaps some kind of external agency or intelligence trying to interact with me. These dreams were utterly lucid – I was entirely self aware, in control of myself and able to make deliberate choices. There was also total clarity in the content – there was nothing that I needed to interpret. I did not need to dig around for meanings, they were self-evident and there at the surface. If the message is hard to express in our limited language, there may be a symbolic element, but the symbols will make a kind of sense to us. If something beyond us has a message for us, we might trust that it can deliver it in ways we are able to understand.

I think the reality is that most of the time, what most of us experience are navel-gazing dreams that only matter in the context of our own minds and lives. We need to reject the idea of special meaning when considering most dreams, and understand them on a personal level. We need to resist the urge to make more of them so that we have scope to recognise the few that are truly inspired and really require our attention.

The trouble with interpretation is that, by its very nature, it is a license to make one thing mean another. So, for example I may dream about birds. I know that ancient Druids studied the flight of birds in order to make predictions. Therefore I interpret the dream as an omen. In the dream, the birds circle above me. I interpret this to mean that I have a special destiny and am beloved of the gods. It may be that in truth it is nothing more than the consequence of sleeping through an enthusiastic dawn chorus with my window open. It could be that the birds are flying in circles because I feel trapped and as though my life is going nowhere and that this feeling also prompts me to want to see myself as special as a way out of that trapped feeling. If I let self-indulgence and ego interpret every dream as a message from the gods, I'll find the confirmation I desire, no matter what happens in my dreams. We humans are terribly good at deluding ourselves, especially by seeing the things we most wanted to find.

As a general rule, the more work you have to do on the symbolism in order to interpret it, the more suspect your conclusions probably are. If you wouldn't otherwise think something a good idea, having a dream about it does not make it into a good idea.

The more work you have to do to uncover the secret, magical message of your dream, the more likely it is that you've put it there yourself. You can shoehorn magical interpretations into anything, if you are determined enough. That doesn't make it real. It certainly doesn't make it a good idea, or a helpful thing to be working with. It's also worth considering that if we are imagining magic where there is none, we are probably missing out on all the real stuff. We're missing out on the small wonders, beauties, mysteries and joys of our actual lives. If we're chasing ideas of wonder and inspiration, we're probably missing actual opportunities for these where they manifest in our dreaming and waking lives alike. When we feed our self-importance at the expense of reason, we do ourselves no favours at all.

Assume that if a truly magical dream came to you, then you would have the insight to recognise it as such. If in doubt, assume it wasn't something innately magical. Being Pagan does not mean you are either entitled or required to have profound and magical dreams every night. However, in accepting ourselves as just another flawed, messy human, not always that special and not singled out by the gods, we can live much calmer, happier lives and be more open to the small wonders that might indeed come our way.

No Right Answers

Dreams are not like exam papers. There are no right and wrong interpretations. There is simply what we do with whatever we get, and whether we find that useful.

Dreams are fluid and flowing things. They aren't always literal or linear, and they aren't always meaningful or coherent. About the only things dreams can be relied upon to do, is suggest an absence of certainty. We can use dreams to explore our inner lives, reflect on our problems, aid us in our learning, fire our imaginations and generally enrich us. About the least helpful thing we can do with dreams is to come at them with dogma. If we insist on a meaning, or in interpreting in certain, rigid ways, all we do is reduce our options. We may narrow our dreaming experience by being dogmatic in our thinking. The more open minded we are able to be, the more able we are to work productively with our dreams.

The only measures of success with dreamwork are how we

feel about what we do, and what else that feeds into. How much does dreamwork help us in our waking lives? Good sleep is important for health, so just making sure that bad dreams do not disturb our sleep has obvious utility. We can use our dreams to monitor and explore our emotions and as a playground for the imagination. We can make dreaming an aspect of our spiritual journey, and seek insight through our dreaming experiences.

If dreamwork enriches or enhances your life in some way, that means whatever you are doing is right for you. If we get it wrong, we will perhaps stay in places of unresolved conflict, denial or delusion. We may obsess in unhealthy ways, find new things to worry about, or new ways to mislead ourselves. Only we can judge our relationship with dreaming and determine whether it is doing us any good.

All spiritual work, all psychological work, all self-help, personal growth and creative development depends on self-honesty. If we set out to delude ourselves, nothing can help us. Only by working with integrity, authenticity, self-honesty and a real desire for insight, do we create a space in which we are able to learn. If our greatest desire is to feel special and important, we will struggle to move beyond that in order to face who we truly are and explore who we could be.

Ask what your dream interpretations do for you. Ask whether the ideas that emerge from dream interpretations are helpful, or self-indulgent. Ask what purpose this work serves in your life. Know thyself.

Chapter Six

Developing Dreamwork

Dreams are highly responsive to our paying attention to them. I've seen it suggested that this means dreamers with a therapist can see their dreams change to fit the paradigm said therapist works in. This is not surprising, given that dreams are usually a conversation we are having with ourselves. If we are having that conversation with other people, that's going to have an influence too, and we may come up with dreams specifically to express something to any reliable audiences we have. In some ways this developing of a shared language can enable communication, but at the same time it can be at the risk of losing something individual.

The more attention we pay to our dreams, the more likely we are to remember them. The more we think about our personal symbolism, the more likely we are to keep using the same symbols in dependable ways. It is a bit like inventing a private language for yourself, and the more you invest in this, the more you will tend to get out of it. The more seriously we take our dreams, the more likely it is that our dreams will have something significant to say to us because we have deliberately opened them up as a channel for communicating with ourselves, and perhaps also with others.

Paying attention to dreams can result in having greater self-awareness within dreams. We become more able to control our actions, may be able to recognise that we are dreaming, and may be able to change or leave the dream at will. This makes us much less vulnerable to nightmares. For the person who wishes to live honourably, being able to carry that deliberately honourable behaviour into dreams may be a great asset. If our sleeping minds betray our waking preferences, that can be really uncomfortable. There are many good reasons for wanting to act when asleep as we would when awake. The issue here is that if we achieve that by squashing some aspect of self, it may be a temporary, illusory success, at best.

The easiest way of working with dreams is to simply pay attention to them when you remember them. Small acts of noticing, considering and reflecting create more of a place for dreams in our lives and make them more available to us. Whatever we think about, we reinforce inside our minds. Thoughts are like pathways through the brain, and the more we go in a given direction, the better established that 'pathway' becomes. This is part of how learning works and key to developing skills. If you can do something without thinking about it, this will usually be because you've spent many hours thinking about it a great deal. Therefore, remembering and thinking about dreams will reinforce our dreaming and our ability to recall what we have dreamed about. This simple engagement will, over time, slightly modify our minds so that it becomes easier for us to remember dreams.

If you are interested in serious dreamwork, try to allow yourself a few minutes of reflection each morning in which to recall your dreams. Staying in bed is best, but any quiet reflection while getting up will have a value. If, on waking, you make an effort to recall your dreams, you have the best chance of remembering something. You may not recall entire dreams, but this is fine. Anything you can recall at this point you will probably remember into the day, giving you more scope to come back and ponder the dream later. Again, with practise we get better at recalling dreams, catching wisps of memory and pulling back something a little more substantial.

If you are able to wake naturally, this is a great help because it enables your body to complete its natural cycles. Being woken from a dream can be disorientating, and while it can improve the likelihood of remembering, the trade-off isn't really worth it. If we shatter a dream, we do not find how it would have ended naturally and if the dream is part of an intellectual process, breaking it part way through does not help us much. Again, this is about treating your dreams as inherently valuable rather than as something to be played with for amusement alone. Deliberately setting alarms to try to wake yourself up from dreams is a disruption of your sleep and dreaming that will do you far more harm than good.

Dream Diaries

One of the best ways of forming a good working relationship with your dreams is to keep a dream diary. Have a notebook dedicated to the purpose, and keep it, and a pen, next to your bed. On waking, jot down the date and whatever you can remember of the dream, in as much detail as appeals to you. Whatever strikes you as being most relevant, is most relevant.

We typically go through two periods of four-hour sleep cycles during the night, if we are allowed to sleep naturally, and give ourselves enough time. There is considerable evidence to suggest that, prior to industrialisation, people more normally experienced these two-sleep cycles as distinct, with a gap of perhaps a few hours between each bout. It is this habit of night waking, for example, that allowed a monastic tradition of having prayers in the middle of the night. It seems that most of our ancestors would have had two dream periods, with a wakeful time in between. Waking in the darkness, there would have been plenty of opportunity to reflect on dreams, or to discuss them. Prayer, contemplation, conversation and lovemaking also seem to have featured as normal uses of the wakeful time, with people even reported as getting up and going out to visit neighbours! Given that our pre-industrial ancestors had no street lighting, being abroad in the wakeful time between dreams must have been a strange, magical period, full of possibility.

We are not so very far removed from our ancestors. Babies

frequently default to this sleep pattern and take a while to learn the less natural, modern approach. If we reduce our exposure to artificial light, we can easily return to pre-industrial sleep patterns. My experience has been that I can surface for a fairly short period in the night and not disrupt my overall sleep pattern in a way that conflicts with what everyone else is doing. Being aware that it is natural wakefulness between sleeps helps me to stay in a dreamy place and return easily to sleeping. During the wakeful time, my mind works in very different ways. I can think about things that are otherwise very difficult for me to consider – seeing my life and experiences from entirely unfamiliar perspectives. I feel that this night-waking experience is changing me. I am calmer, my perspective is developing, I am more resilient, more emotionally stable and more able to think when awake about things I would previously have found difficult.

Often, people who sleep in this natural, two-stage way assume there is something wrong with them and seek medical intervention and sleeping tablets. It looks increasingly as though the wakers may be the healthier group than those whose exhaustion keeps them asleep for six or seven hours at a time. With practise and awareness of what's happening, it is easy to get into the habit of waking between sleep cycles. If you make a habit of keeping a dream diary, you may find (as I have done) that you also wake in the middle of the night and can record dreams from your first sleep cycle, too.

Over time, the dream diary can make visible all kinds of trends in terms of symbols, obsessions, fears, narrative threads, and interests. Looking at a number of dreams gives us a much better sense of what's going on in our minds. We can start to build a sense of the relationships that exist between individual dreams and to chart how our feelings and ideas change over time. Dream diaries can make more apparent the relationships between how we dream and what we're doing when awake. It is worth noting any obvious correlations as they occur, but even if you don't they may become apparent anyway.

Keeping the diary can change how we dream. In my experience, it will encourage settings and scenarios to repeat, with stories growing and developing over many dreams. This can become a really exciting process. With or without the aid of a dream diary, we can revisit dreams and dream settings over many years, even. Our inner worlds can be vast, colourful and exciting places full of adventure and possibility. Keeping note of this can help us notice what we're experiencing, which can in turn enrich our lives. Being conscious of how much we have inside us can add a sprinkle of magic and delight to life, even if you do not think there is anything 'supernatural' about your dreaming.

Keeping a dream diary allows you to confirm and explore any impressions you have about trends in your dreams. It can be a means to charting personal changes and tracking dream ideas. In addition, a diary is also a source of considerable amusement. The content of our dreams is often charming and ludicrous in ways it is pleasant to revisit. Having the diary is a prompt to recalling the dreams you record there, and more broadly a prompt to help dream recollection. Even if you only keep a diary for a short while, or intermittently, it is likely to improve your ability to remember dreams.

We are strange, whimsical, imaginative creatures and a dream diary keeps a small door open onto that side of our natures.

Meditation Before Sleep

Teachers who are serious about meditation often discourage students from attempting to do meditative exercises in bed at night. Sleepiness reduces your concentration and you could nod-off mid process and fail to achieve anything. Many meditation advocates favour being fully alert, awake and able to concentrate when working in this way. Much depends on whether your focus is to develop a disciplined meditation practice, or you are inclined to use meditation as a tool to further some other aim. If you want to use your mind in very deliberate and disciplined ways, the edge of sleep is not the best place to work. If you are interested in the liminal qualities of being between states, this can be a really interesting time to meditate.

If your aim is to work with sleep and dreaming, then meditation can be a tool to that end, even though some forms of meditation may not be best served by the method. The alert meditation approach is one I've never entirely favoured, because my mind is a more interesting place on the edge of sleep, and because meditation tools are so helpful for insomniacs. I've had several patches of troubled sleeping in my life, where meditation has at least helped my body to rest and given me a chance at shutting down my over-active mind. Much of my early interest in meditation grew out of my need for it as a way of coping with insomnia. It is only in more recent years that I've tackled sleeping issues by handling the problems in my lifestyle and environment that were largely responsible. I would therefore advocate caution. It is possible to use meditation as an offset against other problems, but it won't solve everything and you will be better off if you can tackle root causes.

If you are in the process of trying to develop better sleeping habits, it can take a while to figure out what needs to change. Meditation can create a useful space while you are transforming your life and is also good for dealing with occasional sleep disturbances. From this perspective, the whole point is to help yourself settle and rest. Meditation in this context does not have to be a means to an intellectual or spiritual end. It can be enough just to keep your body calm and resting. Meditation can help us calm anxiety, which, if it gets out of hand will make it harder to sleep. The act of undertaking a meditation can sometimes be a lot more relevant than reaching some goal or conclusion. We do not have to achieve a specific endpoint for it to be a rewarding and meaningful experience.

In theory, if you meditate your way towards sleep, this may influence your dreaming. It is not an exact science. In practice, we tend to do most of our dreaming much later in the sleep cycle, so you won't usually move directly from one state to the other, taking your ideas with you. Still, as I'm oft repeating, dreaming is the business of your mind. Other things undertaken with your mind are bound to have an influence. Self-awareness developed through contemplation is going to reduce the unresolved issues your dreaming mind might otherwise try to tackle. Working through anxiety and making peace with problems will reduce the amount of time you spend in dreams running away from dinosaurs and the like. Winding down into a calm, relaxed state improves the quality of sleep. All of this will have an effect on your dreaming.

There are a lot of sound, pragmatic reasons for meditating before sleep, not as a problem solver or antidote to insomnia, but as a way of having a better experience. If you want to undertake elaborate pathworkings with a view to shaping your dreams, you have nothing to lose. It may not work in the way that you intend, of course – especially if you have other things occupying your unconscious mind. Any dreams shaped by meditation are more likely to come in the first sleep cycle, so unless you've developed a habit of waking between sleeps, there's every chance that you won't know if it worked. None of these are reasons to be put off, though.

Whether you manage to influence your dreams directly or not, thinking about dreaming will have some effect. Generally speaking, the more attention you pay to your dreams, the more you will get out of them. Meditating your way towards sleep can help you with this. If you are interested in learning more about meditation approaches for Pagans, you may wish to check out one of my other books – *Druidry and Meditation*.

Working When Waking

The moment when we surface from sleep is when we are most likely to remember our dreams. Consequently, this is one of the best times for many of the dreamwork methods I can offer. Undertaking this in turn depends on your having some time in bed between waking and needing to rise. It is possible to stay in a barely awake state where dreams may linger, but we can also think deliberately about them so long as that gentle and quiet space on the edge of sleep is held for a while.

If you can remember a dream while in this state of consciousness, you have the option of re-imagining it, or coming up with a different ending. While it is thoroughly enjoyable to wallow in the recollection of a good dream, it is also productive to take on the troubling ones in this way. Re-imagining the dream can help overcome any problematic emotional impact it may otherwise have had on you. This time we do not keep running from the monster until our legs quite literally fall off. This time we get a flamethrower and see it off. Working out what the right answer would have been, or how we would prefer to have behaved, can help us overcome any dreams that were uneasy. Reasserting values, and determining preferred outcomes means we are not at the mercy of the dreams. Contemplating our preferred outcomes may help us avoid troubling content in the future. Working through the preferred outcome can also bring up the dream's relevance for waking life, which in turn can be useful.

You can go back and re-imagine doing and saying the right things in whatever way makes sense to you. You can also re-write the actions and words of others, you can change the rules of the dream's reality, and make it work for you. Sometimes it's obvious what needed to be different, sometimes figuring this out is an important process. Either way, you might want to come back later and think about the differences between what you wanted, or needed, and what you actually got. Those differences can be informative, and the more honest we can be with ourselves in this process, the more useful it is.

Sometime it is possible to fully drop back into a dream. Sometimes it happens by chance, but it can become easier with practise and the habit of reimagining. Again it depends on surfacing and being able to re-enter sleep, so this has particular relevance for anyone trying to adopt a more traditional two sleeps approach. The more aware you are of what you have dreamed and how you wanted it to go, the greater your chances of being able to change the dream on returning to it. The more work you do with dreams at the point of waking, the greater the odds of your being able to drop back into dreams in a productive way. Whether we dream properly at this point, or daydream along the edges of sleep, this revisiting can help resolve issues and is a great mood improver if the original dream wasn't so good.

What are we doing during this work? At the surface, we're just making ourselves more comfortable with the dream. If an uneasy dream is underpinned by a real world problem, then imagining we've got a flamethrower isn't going to make the real problem go away. However, in picturing ourselves turning on the source of anxiety and challenging it, we've entered a conversation with ourselves. We've answered that unconscious scream of, 'Danger!' with a message that says, 'We can deal with this problem.' That can be a small first step to sorting your problem out, so long as you follow through on it in other ways, too. Rather than letting anxiety run unchecked, you are encouraging yourself to think that solutions are available, and to start imagining them. While it would not be advisable to use a flamethrower on a problem person in your life, the metaphor moves you towards thinking about what you could use.

Changing the dream can be a way of changing our patterns of thinking and habitual emotional responses. Thoughts, feelings and actions all form reciprocal loops in our waking life, shaping, reinforcing and enabling each other. It is very easy to get trapped in such circles. Generally speaking, it is easier to change thoughts and behaviour than it is to directly alter our emotions. Re-entering a dream intent on getting a different outcome, is one of those rare spaces where it is fairly easy to change how you feel. You're still engaging with the issue raised by the dream, and you are engaging symbolically on the dream's terms, not directly with life issues. This can sometimes make it possible to change how we react. It may be that the dream is the first place you are able to stop running away and face what comes, and that having made this break, you are then able to think differently about waking issues.

Dreamworking on the Edge of Sleep

If you practise dreamwork on waking and meditate before sleeping you will become more aware of how your mind works along the edges of sleep. This is fascinating territory and I can recommend taking the time to explore it. There are some people who seem to go to sleep quickly and who may not have as much opportunity to play with their own consciousness as a consequence. Some of us take a long time to settle. However, rapid settling into sleep may be largely a consequence of the exhaustion inherent in modern lifestyles. Having more time in bed can give you a lot more scope. Working spiritually before and after sleep, and potentially in the night as well if you get into the habit of waking, you will come to know your own modes of thinking and discover what best suits you.

I have found, over years of exploration, that mental states are available to me at these times, which are unlike anything that happens when I'm fully awake. I am capable of thinking and feeling things that are not possible in the same way at other times. When I am able to actively engage with being in an edge-of-sleep state, the boundaries between dream and imagination are blurred. I can experience fragmentary dreaming interspersed with more conscious thought. When I manage a two-sleep night, the waking period in the middle allows me to think in ways that just aren't available to me during the day. I am particularly able to sit with, reflect on and digest big emotional shifts and changes. This makes me considerably more able to handle bigger life issues, and I have also found it to be good emotional healing time. It is my suspicion that we really need this time, that it allows us to do important personal work, and that modern life has robbed us of something critically important by making this period of night waking less available.

While I will not make any wild claims about the significance of being in these between-states, I can say that it feels magical. This is a time that lends itself to creative and magical thinking. There's a sense of openness and possibility. I often find myself feeling more certain about how things are, what my options are, and what I should be doing during this time, but that may be entirely personal. This is a liminal time, and in Celtic tradition, the liminal is inherently magical. We might also be able to arrange our sleeping time at different points in the year so we either wake or go to sleep with the twilight, matching our inner liminal space to the transitional times in the day. Where I've managed to do this, I've found it very powerful. I think edge-of-sleep work is worth cultivating purely for that sense of magical possibility, which is good to have in its own right regardless of whether it takes you anywhere else.

In this, as in all things, I must counsel against over-interpretation. Enjoy the experience for what it is, but never forget that dream states are full of phantasms. That something seems certain on the edge of waking proves nothing. If you start getting feelings of superiority, supernatural powers and uncanny insights, it is as well to take a break, or balance this time against something that will help you maintain a sense of perspective. In the realm of dream, we all have the capacity to be monarchs, superheroes, demigods... and the more adept we become at this, the greater our need for balancing that out in some way. I find there's nothing like cleaning a toilet or washing socks to stop me from settling into any delusions of grandeur!

Magic on the Edge of Sleep

As the previous description suggests, the edge of sleep is an innately magical time when it is still possible to focus the mind and to think in ways that are otherwise unavailable. If you are engaging in any kind of will-working, this can be an interesting time to explore. While the mind is inherently more unruly at this time, it is also more creative, and more able to think in transformative ways. This is particularly true if you are working to change something within yourself.

If your magical practice involves complex ritual or the need to work in a tightly held circle, then edge of sleep is not a suitable time for you. If you favour more improvised forms of magic, are working lightly on ongoing change, not big, dramatic projects – so that you do not worry so much about risks, or have an established approach to otherworldly possibilities already – this time can serve you well.

If visualisation is part of your magical work, then edge of sleep times may really lend themselves. In this between place when we are closer to dreams, that which we visualise can take on a life of its own, and this can be advantageous. However, if the visualisation gets away from you – as it can do when the mind is less inclined to be disciplined – things can get interesting! I would suggest that if you need absolute control over the details, edge of sleep working is not for you. If you are working with broader intentions and ideas, edge of sleep working can bring richness and insight to the work, and open up new ways forwards. If you would benefit from the input of the unexpected, and do not want to just re-enact the conscious script you had planned, the edge of sleep can be a time when it's easier to let something else in.

Magic undertaken along the edges of sleep feels more real –

perhaps because our whole relationship with reality is different at this time. In some ways this is an advantage – that sense of power and certainty is a great enabler, and magic you do not entirely believe in is unlikely to work. The phantasms that thrive along the edges of sleep are not wholly benevolent and we can be easily persuaded to mislead ourselves. Do the work, but do not always believe everything that the work tells you!

If this line of exploration appeals to you, and chimes with something in your own approach to magic, I would recommend moving slowly. Take small acts of will, intention and visualisation to the edge of your sleeping – start with things that you don't need to be in total control of. Sometimes it is useful to work more speculatively. All forms of divination are speculative – the whole point is that you don't have the conscious answer when you start. If you need to make a change, widen an understanding, bring something new into the world and you don't really know what shape it should take, then the edge of sleep can be a good place to start exploring.

On the whole I favour this approach to magic and thinking because I know my conscious, reasoned decisions are not always my best ones. Leave my waking mind to sort it all out and the odds are I will figure out how to work harder and do more. Let my unconscious mind in on the game and I'm more likely to spot when something is futile or taking me in the wrong direction. The conscious mind is more likely to keep us doing what we always do; the unconscious can throw up surprises. When you're looking for insight and inspiration, getting the conscious, rational process to shut up for a while is often a great advantage, and it just doesn't do its thinking well on the edge of sleep. By contrast, the emotional, irrational, creative part of the mind is totally at home in this environment and will sing.

If your magic is primarily about will, control, focus and crafting change in a very deliberate way, edge–of-sleep working will be of little use. If you favour something wilder, more exploratory, seeking inspiration and experience rather than aiming for goals, the edge of sleep is the perfect place to play.

Lucid Dreaming

All too often, lucid dreaming is held up as the aim of dreamwork, alongside interpretation. This is not going to be a balanced section full of carefully weighed up pros and cons. The deliberate quest for control over the self and the dream experience is a project a lot of people clearly find attractive, but I think this is more about ego than growth. Plenty of books exist to make the case for deliberately seeking lucid dreaming as a goal in its own right. I do not think it is a productive thing to chase for its own sake and will lay out the thinking behind this assertion.

A lucid dream is a dream in which the dreamer has control. The level of control can vary from awareness you are dreaming, through control over your own actions, to an ability to control the entire setting and chain of events. Any dream work will increase the likelihood of knowing you are dreaming and having some control over your actions, just because you are setting out to be a more active participant. That in itself is no bad thing, because it doesn't tie you into a lucid state. You still have room to not be lucid when you need it, and you aren't discouraging your mind from expressing things to you. However, there are techniques out there for training the dreaming mind to reliably create lucid experiences of dreaming.

It may well be that highly disciplined spiritual work will ingrain itself so deeply into a person that this manifests in dreaming. It may be that your character is so coherent, your self-honesty so pure, that you do not fragment into shadow selves while asleep. If your dreams are lucid as a consequence of being a clear, lucid and self possessed person, I assume that's fine. I'm speculating because this is not something I have achieved for myself.

I very much doubt that reverse engineering would work in

this context. I do not think you can create an enlightened mind by controlling the content of your dreams. More likely this approach will just allow you to develop and maintain controlling habits. You may be tempted to avoid challenges and to ignore troublesome parts of life and self. Most of our best work will be done in the uncomfortable boundaries, so too much comfort can be a real obstacle to growth and learning.

We are encouraged from an early age to be competitive and to achieve, ticking boxes as we go. Lucid dreaming offers itself as a skill to master, a thing we can say we are able to do. Thus it is attractive to an ego that needs bolstering. It is a thing we can feel important about. We can mistake the tool for the end goal – just as interpretation is not a result, so lucid dreaming is not an achievement. What matters is how we use these things, and as soon as they become goals to attain, we can be distracted from whatever value the approach might have offered us. The ability to have lucid dreams is one of the few things about dreaming we can try to compete over or use for one-upmanship, which is a reason to be wary of our own motives if it's something we are keen to do.

Most of the time, everything we dream about can be understood as being a part of us. If we want more control over what shows up during that process, it means we will be shutting down unwanted aspects of self that wanted to make their presence felt. Silencing aspects of self is not healing, not nurturing and not really doing ourselves any favours. Getting control of the dream does not translate neatly into controlling problem issues when awake. This is just a method of deliberate repression. I firmly believe that control is seldom the answer, and never the whole answer. The challenges we all face require us to grow, adapt and change. We need to reflect on our experiences and understand them. Sometimes we have to work things through before we can let them go. Making peace with an issue is usually a process and not always comfortable. If you are interested in getting more control of your dreams, consider why. What do you want to change about them? What do you want to hide from yourself? Is there some better way of approaching the problem?

I've written already about going back into dreams to re-imagine them in a more lucid way, but there are differences between this approach and full-on lucidity. In the reworking method, you deal with the raw material your sleeping mind created, which gives you room for the unwelcome and difficult things to make themselves known. Consciously revisiting that material is an act of welcoming the unwelcome, facing up to it and making room to deal with it. Even if you go back and resolve the dream more comfortably, you aren't shutting down the experience, but making a space for it. This in turn opens the way for dealing with things. Total control over dreaming gives us the scope to suppress anything we don't want to deal with.

Western culture is relentless in telling us that the rational mind knows best. Reason and logic are championed while feeling and intuition are held suspect. What could be worse than to be irrational? And yet, we are not wholly rational creatures and will make many of our most important decisions for less than perfectly rational reasons. Dreams are one of the few spaces where the intuitive side of self still gets to exist. I think we shut that down at our peril. Lucid dreaming can be a colonization of the wild dreaming space by the conscious, rational mind and that's something I am uneasy about.

What happens if we insist on forcing our rational, waking consciousness into the irrational fabric of our dreams? What can it possibly do but narrow our options? In doing this, we may sacrifice our scope for wild, intuitive leaps and freeform thinking, shut down our symbolic expression and our unrestricted creativity, in favour of giving more time and space to everything we already know. If we allow our conscious selves to take charge in dreams, we may easily reduce our scope to learn. Yes, perhaps we can do anything we can imagine, but then we're

limited by our conscious imaginations, which are never as interesting as the chaos and mayhem of less fettered dreaming.
However good your conscious imagination is, the odds are your
unconscious still has more to offer.

It may be more comfortable to control our dream behaviour
and deny the things our dream self might otherwise do. In
dreams we may exhibit behaviour that would shame or condemn
us if we acted that way when awake. We all have darker threads
in the weave of self. We all have shadows and personal demons.
Silencing them does not make them go away. Facing our demons,
and our demon selves, we can get them into perspective, learn
how to befriend them or at least gently remove the worst of the
pointy teeth. Too much lucid dreaming can rob us of these
options.

At least if we let our wild, irrational, unacceptable selves
roam free in dreams, they might not pop up unexpectedly in
waking life. Giving safe space to the unacceptable self can help
keep us sane and functioning the rest of the time. If we allow
ourselves no space in which to howl and roar, no space for our
shadows, they may devour us in retaliation.

We all have egos, some healthier than others. We have
longings, desires and urges that are not given full satisfaction by
our waking lives. Left to their own devices, our dreams may well
answer this lack. There is nothing wrong with a little fantasy and
self indulgence. Imagining life as it would ideally be can make it
a good deal easier to bear the life you actually have, and can help
you move towards your aspirations. However, anything taken to
excess can become counter-productive.

If we seek full control of our dreaming – not just our own
actions, but the whole show – what will we do with that
achievement? To what degree will we let the demands of our
egos take over? How much time will we give to indulging our
fancies? Will the scope for answering every need in dreams
impact on how we live our waking lives? If we do work on issues

or challenges, or things we needed to learn, will we pick our arena well by picking deliberately? Our unconscious minds may make better decisions about where the need for urgent action lies.

What does it do to us, if we gain total control of our dreaming realities? It might be a charming playground, and we do spend a lot of our lives there. The person who gains absolute control of their dreaming reigns as a superpower in their own tailor-made universe. If you already believe that we make our own reality, this may appeal to you. I have deep misgivings about it. This way lies self-delusion, narcissism, solipsism and other kinds of insanity. What we get with total control of our dreams is the option of wallowing freely in our fears, assumptions, desires and fantasies, unchecked. Not even our own unconscious mind is permitted to challenge what the conscious ego prefers to think about. And if everything is of my making, where is the room for the numinous? Where is the space for something other than me, more than me, to enter my dreaming? Our own godhood in the private universe of our dreams would, I think, be a lonely and unfulfilled condition to achieve.

Of course if you are profoundly wise and spiritual, you might take control of your dreams to wholly benevolent effect. It is my assumption that, if I ever become as wise and spiritual as all that, my dreams will not need conscious controlling. Instead, at that point the harmony in my waking life, the balance within my psyche, the resolution of my conflicts and the peace made with my fear will have already done the work. When there is no conflict between conscious and unconscious, when the rational and the emotional are truly integrated, what could possibly happen in my dreams that I would need to control?

This is something to look forward to, for when I am much, much older. In the meantime, I have a lot of waking work to do, and dreaming to do before I get to that place of true equilibrium.

Lucid dreaming might look like a short cut, or a prize, but I think it is just another way of fooling ourselves. There is far more to dreaming than our conscious engagement. Sometimes, forgetting is the most important thing that happens. Sometimes, not knowing is fine. Not all of who we are is meant to be at the surface and exposed to bright light all of the time.

Chapter Seven

Exploring a Dream Diary

I have mentioned before that keeping a dream diary is a great way of interacting with your dreams. However, if you are not in the habit of writing or keeping a diary, this may seem either odd or intimidating. Recording any aspect of our lives for posterity by writing it down gives it a sense of importance, and if we are not confident about ourselves, that can feel like it is too much. Taking your dreams seriously is key to good dreamwork. Treating your dreams (no matter how odd or fragmentary they are) as something worth writing down is an expression of taking the experience seriously. You do not have to write reams of poetry, you do not need to be equal to magnificent insights. It is enough to invest in a notebook and have a go. That action alone changes things and puts you on a path.

The following pages offer a few weeks from a dream diary that I kept specifically as part of the process of writing this book. Alongside the dreams are my best attempts at making sense of these dreaming experiences. One of the things this demonstrates is the important relationship between waking activity and dreams. Only I know what events in my life, historical, contemporary and anticipated, may pertain to a dream. Reading it as an observer, you have no idea what in my life may connect with my dreaming, and that's important to recognise because it underlines the weaknesses of conventional dream interpretation. Of course I may get the matching of experience to dreams wrong, and assume connections that do not exist, read in things I want to see or wilfully ignore awkward issues. If I'm in denial about something, how am I to tell? However, no one else has the same degree of access to the inside of my head, or to my experiences. Anyone trying to interpret dreams without the context is bound to struggle.

This is ultimately a personal process, and only as useful as we permit it to be. Sometimes, the dream diary permits us to look back over our dreams in a more objective way and with distance and overview. If we are to be our own priests and priestesses, we need to learn how to take on the role of wise advisor in our own lives, rather than looking to someone else for guidance and interpretation. That means facing up to our potential hubris and delusions, facing the things we might prefer not to think about, and working to be utterly self-honest. It is not an easy path to walk, but in the study of our own dreams we have a relatively safe and boundaried space in which to tackle all these issues.

Dream interpretation, when undertaken on your behalf by a book, or by someone else, will tend to fall back on obvious cultural symbolism. This can tend to reduce our nuanced personal symbols down to the most obvious and most limited interpretations, discouraging us from looking at what exactly we are playing out. Thus anything longer than it is wide will start to look far too much like a penis. So many symbols depend on cultural context – in Western thought, white is the colour of life and black the colour of death, but in Taoist thinking, the reverse is true.

When it comes to interpretation, all we have are our beliefs or best guesses about meanings. As the symbols are ours, what we think and feel in response to them must be our best guide. Someone interpreting for us brings their belief along, where that may have no relevance to our symbolic language. After all, if I dream about being back at school and turning up naked to a maths lesson, whether or not that's a nightmare may depend entirely on how attractive or alarming I considered my maths teacher to be! If I am in denial about lusting after my maths teacher, and take this to a dream interpreter who associates maths with rationalism, and rationalism with patriarchal oppression, we are unlikely to come to similar conclusions about what it all meant.

While I was keeping this diary, there were nights when I did not remember dreams, or I forgot to write them down. There were dreams that defied description, as well, and I did not try to include them. A couple were too personal to be shared. This is my diary and it is my choice what to represent, what to withhold and what I am willing to explore – and the same is true for all such diaries. Self-honesty is good, but so is being compassionate with yourself if you aren't necessarily ready to tackle everything right now. There is no requirement to write everything, or to keep a dream diary diligently every day. It needs to fit in around your life and keeping it when it occurs to you may be the best approach.

November 26

Dream: I was learning how to deep sea dive, so was in the bottom of a very deep swimming pool in lead boots, but had no air supply. I felt I had to try to take the boots off and swim to the surface. I wasn't having any trouble breathing underwater, but still thought there was a risk of drowning. My instructor was not impressed by this and had to go down to retrieve my boots. I knew I should have had the Victorian-style divers' helmet, which was inexplicably absent. I felt excited about the prospect of wearing one, and remembered seeing just such a diving suit as a child. I also remembered that normally such suits had an air pipe.

Interpretation: Mild anxiety elements around being out of my depth and not properly equipped. Being able to breathe under-water seems significant because there is no real danger to me in this situation. It is interesting that I can do something that normally I couldn't. It suggests I am worrying unnecessarily – which is always likely given how I am. I'm excited about the Steampunk credibility around Victorian diving gear – image, authenticity, coolness, there are reasons for me to feel positive about this sort of aesthetic. However, it's not a costume I had previously considered attractive, and I was actually alarmed when I saw said gear as a child. There's an interesting perception shift in the dream in terms of re-writing a historical experience.

I had started writing a new novel on the day before the dream, (a bit in-at-the-deep-end) and had seen a Doctor Who episode featuring aliens whose big heads may have informed the diving helmet.

November 27

Dream: I dreamed about Green Party policy, and about my work.

Interpretation: I had been at a Green Party meeting that evening. Consolidation of learning in action!

November 28

Dream: Toilet doors that do not lock, or that open into other toilets. I go to a medical centre where I cannot explain what the problem is. I cannot remember where I live or which school my child attends, leading to social embarrassment.

Interpretation: All standard anxiety tropes for me, and I had been worrying about work and money that evening. Fear of public humiliation, fear of getting things wrong and being incompetent, also fear of dealing with powerful professionals. These are all waking-life issues for me.

November 30

Dream: Tom (my husband) and I were trying to watch an 18 rated film. Other people kept coming in – usually my family. No space, no privacy. At one point we were in a spare room at my deceased grandmother's house – she was present, alive and did not want us there.

Interpretation: We had been having trouble with a heater and had to talk to the landlord. I wonder if not owning the place I live in is more of an issue for me than I had previously thought. Being able to own and therefore control a space seemed key in the dream. I am answerable to others over how I privately use this space. A desire to be more in control, less answerable to anyone, is suggested. Historically I have been deliberately disempowered by others around control of space issues. Perhaps I am still feeling insecure about that.

December 3

Dream: Fragments of dreams in which I was an artist and something trashed the jumper I'd been wearing the previous day. Hard to recall.

Interpretation: No obvious significance on the art side. I'm not an artist. I can use clothes to talk to myself about identity and I've been low for some days, the shredded jumper would seem to be a reflection of that.

December 5

Dream: I dream I am singing and playing the violin with a short, elfin woman who I've never met before. She is famous (in the dream) and we're doing a radio interview after which there's a strange and sometimes alarming ride to the sea in a steam-powered car shaped like a tank, but with no hull. Tom may have been driving it. Lots of colours in this one, very vivid. None of the places or people were familiar aside from Tom and, later, an old school-friend. By this point in the dream I could not remember who I was or what I was supposed to be doing.

Interpretation: There was a steam-powered car in the fiction I'd been writing that day, so that was clearly on my mind. I'd also been thinking about going to the Folk Awards in February and from there on a daytrip to Brighton – somewhere I've never been. That may explain the journey and the sea. I may have substituted the school friend for the Brighton friend, possibly as a mental shortcut. I'm not very good at faces.

The loss of memory around identity is something that regularly features for me. I know this is significant and I am not sure how to make sense of it. This may be about underlying anxieties. It may suggest periods of flux and change, or a need for change.

(I note, coming to this months later in re-draft, that I was probably in the early stages of burn out and building towards a huge meltdown that happened a couple of months later, and that these may have been early warning signs which, at the time, I did not spot. I had a lot of issues around needing to reclaim identity and a sense of direction, which I've since been working through.)

December 7

Dream 1: Someone I knew had locked me in my bedroom, and refused to let me leave. I was trying to get my phone to text for help. When I did eventually escape, I was able to fly, but they hunted me with guns and I could not fly high enough to get away and was shot.

Interpretation: Said person had a history of being highly critical of me, which does have the emotional effect of shutting me in. The escape route I chose in the dream brought me even greater problems than I already had. As this dream came around the anniversary of a significant event in my life, that it is echoing something from my history seems likely. The 'shut in' symbolism suggests I am thinking about things differently now – now seeing as unacceptable things that in the past I have accepted as things I deserved. On the whole, in my waking life, escaping from the shut room was not as dangerous or damaging as I feared it would be.

As I woke from this dream in the night, I went back and attempted to re-imagine it, and managed not to get shot during my second escape attempt.

Dream 2: I kept finding biting insects with enormous, spiky bodies, clambering over me. They got inside my clothes and laid eggs. They had horns/needles like unicorns but were ugly. They arrived on plant-matter my son had brought into the house.

Interpretation: The cat had suffered a bout of fleas, which may have informed the imagery. I wonder if I had pins and needles during the night as my circulation has been poor lately. Otherwise I have no sense of meaning beyond generic anxiety and discomfort.

Dream 3: I was sat in the back seat of a car. Everyone else got out and the car started moving. I tried to get the handbrake, but it wouldn't work, so I climbed into the driver's seat and tried to control the car as it rolled off down the road. The car turned into a motorbike with no indicators and I was able to bring it to a halt.

Interpretation: I don't drive in real life, and never have, but I have striking dreams about being in the back seats of runaway cars, or obliged to try to drive. I think for me, the car is a symbol of power (other people's) and problematic responsibility (probably mine). Power over me in quite a literal sense around access to transport and my ability to control things can show up here, and that probably relates to the first dream of the night. My ability to take control of things that scare me has been an ongoing issue. Being asked to take responsibility for things that are beyond me has often been a problem in the past. I think driving a car is a shortcut for talking about that.

December 8

Dream 1: Fairly banal and domesticated, revolved around the store posting our missing loyalty card back to us.

Interpretation: We had lost a loyalty card; it was not found and returned to us. All very dull and real life, but I can fret a lot about very small mistakes. I worry when I get things wrong, and the degree to which I worry about things I should be able to shrug off as inconsequential is highlighted by this dream.

Dream 2: Surreal dream involving cysts/boils in the skin that were also stone-built wells in a landscape that also had ink in it that could be spread out through the skin to make tattoos. The shape of the tattoos would then influence how your body worked – tattoos on feet influenced walking and relationship with the land. Lots of blue in the dream. Lots of imagery randomly juxtaposed.

Interpretation: While I have been thinking about getting a new tattoo, I felt this dream went far beyond the mundane. There was a sense of meaning or significance that I can't unravel, a hint of mystery, possibility. Something numinous. Obvious implications for writing and inspiration around the ink in the skin and the exposing of the personal. I tend to associate wells with femininity and sexuality, and tattoos with empowerment and self-possession. As I frequently do not have a good relationship with my own body, there might be something a bit hopeful in the atmosphere of this dream, where something ugly – the cysts/boils turns out to be something beautiful, magical and powerful.

December 10

Dream 1: Someone I know tells me they and their partner are splitting up; I try to persuade them that they ought to move to Stroud.

Interpretation: To the best of my knowledge, this is not even slightly true or at all likely, there may be some wishful thinking on my part though, as I do not get on with the partner in question. It is also indicative of my increasing investment in Stroud as a home for the long term.

Dream 2: I dreamed I was remembering many of my teeth falling out. When I woke I was disorientated because of the high level of sensory content in the dream, which left me feeling like I'd just had most of my teeth fall out.

Interpretation: No idea! All teeth correct and present. This is a frequent kind of dream content for me – I think it is sometimes prompted by my wisdom teeth moving. There is an anxiety component. When I am really stressed I clench my teeth while asleep, and that can become painful, which may again inform my dreaming. There could be combinations of mind and body issues at work here.

Dream 3: I dreamed Tom had come over to visit from Germany, but would be leaving me again shortly, which really upset me.

Interpretation: I was alone in bed when I dreamed this, which is an unusual arrangement. I wonder if the physical awareness of his absence triggered memory of the time we spent apart early on in our relationship. I have no idea why I made it Germany rather than America.

December 11

Dream: I was being forced – entirely against my will – to take part in some sort of cycling event where I would have to take a bike three times round a mountain. It would probably kill me, I knew.

I was struggling to find any trainers to wear and anxious people were telling me I must not do it in the sandals I was wearing. It was also very important that I did not let anyone discover my actual gender, but I have no idea why this mattered! I did find the necessary shoes, though.

Interpretation: There are some parallels between the cycle challenge and some extreme pilgrimage activities I'd read about before sleep, so I think that informed the core narrative of the dream. I can't ride a bicycle, so I'm being asked to do the impossible, and I have uncanny knowledge that it will kill me and that no one must know my gender. In terms of waking life, I feel utterly overwhelmed by the current political situation and ill-equipped to make any difference. If the dream reflects that, then it also suggests that on some level I do think I can step up. In the dream I was uncharacteristically unafraid of the challenge, and of the dangers, which may be a good sign.

December 12

Dream: That Druid Kris Hughes's acolytes were trying to catch me. We could all levitate. I took roofs off buildings in a bid to escape.

Interpretation: Kris Hughes is a lovely chap with whom I had not fallen out in any way any time recently. We had a tiny spat years ago, of no great significance. I have only limited online contact with him most of the time, so there is no obvious explanation for this. However, the following day had a lot of stressy things in it, which I did not know were coming, so it is tempting, with hindsight, to see the dream as a little bit predictive.

I tend to associate flying with how I am feeling spiritually, so the presence of a hostile Druid and the levitation suggests it might be about that. Kris is a Very Important Druid, in terms of the modern movement. Most of the time I am entirely comfortable with being a not-very-important Druid, preferring the reduced authority/responsibility for a start. But I'm not immune to the cries of ego, and of course there are days when I feel resentful over what I am not. Obviously, aiming to be all wise and Druidic does not normally make it easy to acknowledge the flawed human wishes for status, and it remains a difficult thing to admit to. As a Druid, I should be above all of that, surely? But as a human, I am not.

December 19

Dream: He was no one I knew, 18 and pretty with big, dark eyes and he persisted in courting me, despite my age and protests and refused to believe that I could be more than a few years older than him.

Interpretation: There was nowhere obvious for this to have come from. I am hardly youthful seeming, I find it unlikely that anyone much would find me attractive and I cannot imagine what part of my mind conjured the boy – it just isn't how I think about myself. I think the most likely explanation is that it was a form of self-ridicule. I wasn't noticeably attractive to 18-year-olds even when I was that young, I knew it at the time, and it remains obvious. I'm also conscious that if this was someone else's dream I would make entirely different suggestions about how to make sense of it, while I would reject as deluded any bit of me that thought this scenario made any kind of sense.

December 29

Dream: I'm doing my A Levels again, and am failing music because I haven't practised the piano in more than a decade. During the dream it slowly dawns on me that something is wrong with this scenario. I recall that I have a degree, and that I've already taken these exams. I start refusing to go to lessons or to show up at school.

Interpretation: This set-up used to be a standard nightmare for me, but I've not had it for a while. I think this is about my being pushed around by other people, feeling obliged, tested, given hoops to jump through. A sense of having to prove that I'm good enough. Being able to feel I have the right to say no and to choose my own path is an ongoing struggle for me. Remembering who I am, what I've done and what I should not be made to do again seems like a sign of good progress in my waking life.

December 31

Dream: I was pregnant, to Tom and trying to run what was either a trip to London or a bake sale – it was curiously hard to tell! I kept falling over and at one point was face down on the floor, watching a tiny orange creature climb out of a flower. Vivid colours, lots of noise and bodily sensation.

Interpretation: I was not in the least bit pregnant, nor was it at all feasible that I could be. I think it was a body dream caused by actual pain and exhaustion. I tend to dream that I've fainted when I'm really tired and it seems to be a warning sign that I need to take more care of myself and get more rest.

January 1

Dream: I had an option of either going back to live somewhere I lived a while ago, or alternatively of buying my grandmother's old house in Dursley. I didn't want to do either, although both alert me to lost things and people I miss. However, in the dream I felt very strongly that I wanted to stay in Stroud.

Interpretation: Houses are often taken as symbols of self. Those locations both relate to my historical identity, but I think this dream was more about deciding where I belong in a geographical sense. Location also has to do with life choices, my feelings of connection to landscape, and finding somewhere I feel I fit socially. I've spent most of my life not really knowing where I fitted, in any sense, so having that clarity and seeing it show up so clearly even in dreams, is of great importance to me.

(I note later that at the time of this dream I had no awareness that there would soon be an opportunity of buying a place to live, so the sense of foreshadowing is interesting.)

Interpreting the Diary

My short period of dream-diary keeping demonstrates very plainly that I am a worrier. My anxiousness during these few weeks is wholly visible in my dreams, and that's fairly typical of how I had dreamed for years. If anything, I've improved somewhat. The way anxiety impacts on my dreaming, and my life, is much more evident if I track it over time. If I'm not tracking my dreams (as has been the case around the second draft of this book) I tend not to know how frequent my anxiety dreams actually are. It is not a topic over which I am that honest with myself, unless I monitor my dreaming.

There are insecurities I like to think I hide when awake, but which my dreams expose. Not only do I try to present myself to the world as a calm and confident person, but I've taken a 'fake it until you make it' approach to how I think about myself. In many ways this is a productive use of denial because I am only going to change some of these things by doing differently, and if faking it lets me do it, I can move towards being more genuinely relaxed and confident. My dreams do give me an insight into how well I am managing this, and whether my underpinnings are secure, or whether beneath the fake confidence there remains a deep vein of fear and self-doubt.

My imagination, in all its strangeness, shows through clearly in these dreams as do some of my preoccupations. I'm quite obsessive and my dreams tend to reflect whatever is dominating my mind at any given time.

I did not record everything, but I noticed this is because of the frequency with which my dreams during the period of the diary were just messy fragments that defied my best attempts to make sense of them. This is important in its own right. It represents an improvement on the many years where I just had the same, narrow set of anxiety dreams, but at the same time I know I'm not dreaming at full capacity, and that I have things to sort out, and probably ought to rest more than I do. During the time I've been working on this book since keeping the diary, the coherence of my dreams has improved further.

I tend to find that my dreams reflect my emotional life more than anything else. As I am intensely emotional, and many of my choices are driven by my feelings, this comes as no surprise to me. I daydream vividly along the edges of sleep, when I am more and less conscious, and it is not always easy to tell these from 'proper' dreams.

Chapter Eight

Dreams and Magic

Thus far in the book I have taken a fairly rational approach to dreaming, informed by what I know about psychology and the science of sleep. It has been an attempt to rationalise dreaming and relate it to bodily experience, mental processes and emotional life. It is my belief that for the greater part, dreams are just part of normal life, and if normal life is innately mundane, our dreams will simply reflect that back to us.

However, waking life is not always mundane. Those on a creative path and working with the glorious insanity of inspiration have a far more interesting relationship with reality. That includes people who daydream, who invest in the books they read and who make room in their minds for the extraordinary.

Spiritual work tends to lead us away from the mechanistic end of realism. Spiritual truths are not the same as rational truths. Spending time in contemplation, meditation and prayer, in search of the divine and answers to the questions of existence, we change our relationship with reality. If we see the material universe as invested with spirit, awareness, soulfulness and intent, then even when we are thinking about the mechanistic world, we do so in a different way. As soon as you start to perceive trees as distinct individuals with their own living presence, your relationship with reality changes. One can be wholly rational without being soulless. I would argue that being soulful opens us to more possibilities.

If your Paganism takes you into magical practice – be that spellwork, prayer, or a quest to perceive the magical in the mundane, you cease to inhabit a banal reality. For many, the Pagan path is about re-enchantment and learning to feel wonder in face of the material world. If we are walking this path then the odds are that our quest for a more magical understanding of the world will shape our perceptions and our dreams alike.

Seeking the magical and looking for wonder does not have to mean abandoning reason. It's not all dancing unicorns and astral trips to Atlantis. In fact for some of us, it isn't that at all. Re-enchantment can be very much about learning to see the beauty in life as it is lived. Nature is often incredibly beautiful. Life that is touched by love and informed by compassion can be incredibly rich. Thus seeking magic doesn't have to mean some kind of self-indulgent ego trip, or a flirtation with raging insanity. It can simply be an opening of the heart to the very wonderful real world we inhabit. There is nothing banal about real life; it is just that we learn to close down our senses and our minds. We learn not to notice, and not to care. It is our own complacency that gives us banality. Re-enchantment is about learning not to be complacent. All the rest flows naturally from that openness.

Magical dreaming is something that will start to happen for us if we engage with our lives, and with our dreams. It is the process of going deeper in, to find the richness and the resonance. It is the consequence of learning to love what is already present.

Of Gods and Dreams

The interpretations of dreams that see at least some of them as being messages from the divine, the gods, or the ancestors, are an array of understandings that cross cultures, geography and millennia. In addition to this, dreams have also been widely ascribed healing and divination roles. It is worth noting that most often, the ordinary dreams of regular people have not been much in consideration around these kinds of understandings. It seems to be the dreams of priests and sovereigns that are given this kind of weight and viewed as likely messages from the gods. This may be a bias created by the surviving material because there tends to be precious little out there about what ordinary people got up to in most contexts. There is a logic to thinking that if you are powerful, you are more likely to be beloved of/informed by the big gods of your tribe and culture. The Celts seemed to have had a lot of more localised deities, perhaps people with less power had more interaction with smaller, more local gods. I speculate.

Modern Paganism functions in very different ways from much of what we know about ancient Paganism. Many ancient Pagan religions were hierarchical and did have a priesthood. Most people did not self identify as fulfilling the role of priest or priestess, so far as we know. The heroic cultures we tend to hark back to were led by a ruling elite, most were not even slightly democratic, and even Greek democracy was a long way from how we think about democracy today. Our relationships with power, sovereignty and the role of the individual have changed, creating a very different context. Across modern Paganism, individual practitioners are taking on those roles of leadership and sovereignty in terms of attitude and approach. Practices that might once have been elite, become widespread. The culture we exist in creates a totally different context, and we tend to think we hold more power, sovereignty and priesthood in our own lives than peasant ancestors would have done.

Religious dreaming, and receiving dreams from the gods, has most normally been the work of kings, and high-ranking priests. Most historical Paganism was a good deal more formal and hierarchical than anything we practice today. There are many things to be said in favour of this process of democratising spirituality and empowering people to take a more active role in their spiritual lives. The flip side is that we all end up doing the work that would otherwise have been in the hands of trained professionals, with neither the training nor the professional support this really requires, all too often. It is not an easy path to walk.

Does that mean that we should take our dreams as seriously

as an ancient king might have done? In practice most of us do not lead nations or have that much power. Arguably your average modern Pagan has far less power and influence than a Pagan priest of the ancient world. Our individualistic Western culture encourages us to think that we should all be special. Perhaps we don't think that *everyone* is special enough to be getting messages from the gods, but we may be a touch predisposed to thinking that we of course are that special. The gods will have messages for us and want us to do things for them, and therefore will be in touch... it's a tempting line of thought. Does experience bear that out? I would suggest that unless your work takes you into the absolute frontline of a god's area of interest, the odds of hearing from them seem slim. Old deities of warfare, childbirth, poetry and the grain harvest seem unlikely to really care that much about office politics and a trip to the store. Our culture is very different to that of our ancestors, and if we are not dealing with life, death and the natural world in some very immediate ways, how are we even to make sense of the deities associated with such things?

As soon as we postulate that there might be a supernatural aspect to dreaming, we have to wonder about the mechanics that allow messages to enter our minds from elsewhere, as we sleep. How open or closed do we believe ourselves to be? There are no clear answers. Do we see ourselves as closed spheres of consciousness, or somehow connected with other nodes of consciousness? Are we isolated, or part of a web? We absorb many influences in wholly rational ways. We draw in far more raw data via our senses than we are capable of fully processing. We are not entirely closed systems, that much is apparent.

Conventional wisdom at the moment has it that physics shapes reality, and consciousness experiences the results. However, I have encountered an idea called biocentrism, which postulates that the reverse might be true. If consciousness is the starting point of all things and physics simply follows and expresses that, then the whole idea of the permeable mind makes a lot more sense. If it is consciousness, not physics, that underpins everything in a most literal sense, then in the raw consciousness of dreaming, all manner of things may be possible that from a physics-first perspective make no sense at all. This, I must add, is about the worst kind of thing to have in your head when trying to sleep, and I recommend not pondering it when you're working along the edges of sleep.

Where dreamwork is concerned, a lone practitioner may easily over-value the significance of their own dreams, and thus struggle to differentiate between wish fulfilment and divine messages. We don't have the social constructs for sharing our religious experiences with more experienced practitioners, and if online exchanges are indicative, we are not, as a community, terribly open to learning from each other sometimes. The tension between the desire for significance and the frequent reality of our insignificance makes us want to see things that may not be there and resent those who tell us we are fooling ourselves.

I would suggest as a guideline, that if you feel shock, fear, awe, wonder, terror or are otherwise shaken and emotionally overwhelmed, it is worth considering the religious implications of your dreams. If, on the other hand, the dream was nice, comfortable, encouraging or could be described in some other mild and unthreatening language, it is perhaps better ascribed to your own unconscious mind, or to something smaller and closer to home than a major, named deity.

If you are drawn to a pantheon, you will know or can find out which of its gods are relevant to dreaming. In theory, any deity could contact you in dreams, if you believe that is how the world works. If you believe in the literal existence of deities, then you can undertake to relate directly to the gods of dreaming, as well.

You may instead have a more shamanic outlook, and see dreaming as an otherworld in which different spirits can interact. Perhaps your inclinations are more Jungian, and you enter the collective unconscious when dreaming. Equally, you may be an atheist, for whom dreaming is a curious product of biology, only meaningful because we choose to give it meaning. It is important to remember, regardless of which view we adopt, that we do not really know. The atheist perspective may seem the most evidenced, but only holds up if we are right in thinking physics underpins consciousness. If in truth it is the other way round and consciousness is the foundation on which physics stands, then all bets are off. If we can hold our beliefs non-dogmatically, we can learn and adapt when things come along that do not fit tidily into our story and we can be that bit gentler with people who think differently about their experiences.

I do not know what the truth is about the nature of dreams. I am a maybeist. I look at the list I've written above, and I think *yes, all of that may be true! Or may not. Or maybe it's something else entirely.* I cannot, from such a perspective, easily teach anyone a system for working with the gods. But maybe you could find that way of working, and maybe it would make sense for you. Maybe you need to bring your innate shamanism into this practice. Do take some time to consider your responses and also consider why you believe this is how things are, and then consider what you can do with that.

Why would the gods want to talk to us in dreams? Why at this point and not in some more reliable way when we are properly awake, paying attention and more likely to get the message? Dreams tend to be cryptic. Why risk dodgy interpretation rather than give us clear messages and instructions? Why create an approach that has traditionally needed a trained priesthood to make sense of it? I can point at that and show how it gives power and a sense of mystery to priests, serving a human end but not proving divine presence at all. I would suggest that therefore the more work you have to do to interpret the divine message, the less likelihood there is of any divine presence in the first place.

However, that cynicism around human interpretation of

mystical things depends in turn on the assumption that the logic of gods is the same as the logic of the waking human mind, and that our fairly predictable physical world is the important bit. What if that isn't true? What if this material world exists only to give us the means to dream? How would we know? What if the logic and reality of the divine has more in common with, and is more concerned with, sleeping than waking?

I've been watching my dreams for a good 20 years, looking for signs of mystery. I want to find magic and wonder, but in turn that can make me more sceptical about interpreting my experiences. In all of that time, there have been a handful of prophetic dreams, and quite a lot that brought a sense of the numinous and left me feeling profoundly inspired and uplifted. There were a few that suggested deity to me, and that I certainly wanted to believe had deeper significance. Can I trust that? I don't really know. Only one dream over my entire life to date has left me reasonably confident that there had been something divine about it and that was because of the life shattering carnage that came in its wake.

It may be the case that my lack of firm belief means the gods are never going to take much interest in me. Organised religions are quick to tell us that our lack of experiences of the divine are proof not of godly absence, but of our own sins, failures and shortcomings. It's a very convenient explanation. Whether that makes it true or not is a whole other question and there is no coming at this issue without some kind of personal bias.

I still wonder whether that one, stand-out dream was truly an experience of the divine, or whether my wiser and less conscious self had constructed the whole thing to try and alert me to some very real issues. Doubt is a fundamental part of my spiritual life. When we become too absorbed with belief, we risk complacency and error. We risk smug self-importance and adventures in egotism. Dreams do not give us much certainty, and this is perhaps a good thing. There is much to wonder about, make guesses over, and be inspired by, but there will never be absolute clarity of meaning, or perfect certainty about what we experience in that state. There is also a shortage of comfort, reassurance and clear assertions about what we should be doing. Life remains as messy and challenging as it always was. The magical does not translate neatly into magical solutions.

Healing Dreams

'Magic' is all too often the term we use when we just can't explain something. There is far more to magic than our incomprehension. Sleeping has great restorative effects on mind and body alike. It is a blessed state, for entirely pragmatic reasons.

There is no need for much belief in any kind of magical process when considering the possible healing power of dreams. We know that the mind uses sleep as a time to sort out and store information, the impact of sleep on learning makes this evident. Sleep is an important part of how we make sense of challenges. When it comes to times of trauma, emotional distress or significant upheaval, there is always work to be done making sense of experiences and learning from them. We learn about the world, and we learn about ourselves. We either make the experience part of our worldview, or we reject it as an anomaly.

For example, in times of bereavement, we have to absorb the absence, and the grief of it, and understand what it means for us in our day-to-day lives. We also have to re-imagine the future without the missing loved one as a physical presence. All the things we will now not get to do, or say, have to be adapted to, and the more invested we were, the more painful this process will be. That's a great deal of rethinking to do, and not all of it will happen consciously.

We handle trauma better when we are able to learn it as an abnormal experience. If we learn to think of trauma as normal, the damage we suffer is greater, and it takes a lot of very deliberate work to undo that. Unlearning anything is a difficult process. Extra time spent asleep, and dreaming, can be a great help with this and people who are distraught often find a need to sleep more.

Sleep also allows the body to heal, and rest is a vital part of overcoming illness. There are many physical processes going on when we are at rest and, while dreaming is an important part of this, it is also important to remember there are limits in terms of what it can do for us. We should not expect dreams to magically heal us from the consequences of our ongoing lifestyle choices. If we do not take care of our bodies, no amount of magical thinking can be expected to compensate for the implications of this. Any undertaking, magical or spiritual, can be used to good effect to support whatever else we do, but it is unwise to expect any such approaches to do the whole job for us. Dreams are more reliably used as ways of noticing what's happening with our overall health or lack thereof, than as a foolproof method for curing all ills.

If we are seeking healing through dreams, then simply devoting more time to good sleep will be productive. It is important not to focus too consciously on the things we want to fix. Contemplating pain, loss, sources of fear and other difficulties will help you stay awake, and feeding your anxiety will not help you to sleep. It is more effective to use relaxing techniques so that you go into sleep states as calmly as possible, and just give yourself permission to work on issues while sleeping. It's surprisingly effective just to decide that you are open to the possibility of a healing dream, and then letting go to see what comes, rather than trying to force something. We don't tend to heal by force, but when the issues are of heart and mind, we can progress simply by letting go a little and trusting ourselves – our conscious and unconscious selves – to find a way forward.

Giving yourself permission to seek a healing dream is also an act of giving yourself permission to heal. Feelings of guilt, shame, failure and responsibility can trap us in places of pain in part because we do not forgive ourselves for perceived error and are thus unable to get over what has happened. We can feel like we do not deserve to heal, or that our own wellbeing is not important enough to merit having time and energy invested in it. There is a great deal of power in simply permitting yourself to work a thing through with a view to moving beyond it. Just in asking ourselves for healing dreams, we take a small but very important step in the right direction.

When we resolve something in a dream, or more likely, we take a small dream step forward towards resolution, that can feel magical. Release and relief are powerful experiences in their own right. It is possible to find both through dreaming. Cathartic expressions, the space to howl our grief, the room to get angry, the chance to re-imagine – there are many things dreams can enable us to do that aid in the healing process. Exactly how this works in practice depends a lot on the precise details of our circumstances. However, working with our dreams, being open to what they tell us and making time for them can be a great help in dealing with things that may otherwise seem beyond us.

In making time for sleep and rest, we are caring for ourselves, and that self-care alone can be incredibly powerful. There is self-valuing inherent in self care, and allowing ourselves that can be transformative. Time given to rest allows us to access a range of different mental states – relaxed but conscious, unconscious, and the wakeful time in the night about which we know so little as I write this. Giving ourselves opportunity to think in different ways opens the door to insight, fresh perspectives and self honesty – an array of tools that equip us to deal more effectively with our waking issues. There are many mechanisms available to us, but no matter what our issues and our exact approach, good sleep is innately healing.

Dreaming as a Spiritual Practice

The dreaming mind is in many ways a reflection of our waking minds. Who we are, what we believe in, our impulses and our honour will manifest in our dreams. Alongside this we also get things we've read and seen, bodily urges and experiments, the fruits of our imaginings, our doubts and our fears. The vast majority, if not all, of the content of our dreams, is us. Part of what makes them confusing is that it is seldom perfectly clear which bit or bits of us are manifesting and why – especially when we are experimenting with things we long for or fear may be true. The less self-aware we are, the less sense our dreams are likely to make. The less self-discipline we have, or self-acceptance, the more likely we are to have dreams that manifest things we aren't comfortable with. The more in denial we are, the more we repress, the more deluded we are, the more likely our dreams are to be problematic or confusing.

Having a robust and dedicated spiritual practice gives a person mental discipline. We cultivate virtues in keeping with our path – compassion, creativity, honesty, fidelity, patience, generosity, self-reliance, courage, respect, wisdom... Paganism is very much about virtue-led ethics and the personal cultivation of the specific virtues we have chosen to individually focus on, defines us in our personal path. When the virtues we seek to develop are really embedded in our hearts and minds, we will manifest and uphold them asleep as readily as we do when awake. If, for the greater part, your dreaming self upholds the values of your waking self, this will be because your spiritual life is truly central to your life. You believe what you claim to believe, and you feel what you claim to feel.

If yours is a path of hot air and ego, your dreaming will not reflect the virtues you have claimed for yourself when awake. If you are faking the appearance of spirituality because you think it makes you look good, you want to fit in, or because you long for something that is absent from your life, you might not be getting the glowing, spiritual dreams you want and imagine you should have.

Taking on a new virtue to cultivate, there will of course be a transition period, as we go from cautious or fearful to learning how to manifest courage, for example.

As I write this book, I am trying to cultivate open hearted trust as a virtue, but it's hard because I have many reasons to be mistrustful. It may take me years. I may be better at acting as though I trust people than I am at feeling trust – and when this is part of a process, there's nothing wrong with it not all being tidy. However, it is all too easy to cultivate only the appearance of a virtue and to do so because we want to look good and feel special. In such instances, there is no depth to the work – this is entirely different from what happens with someone who is struggling to make a transition. If there's a lack of real commitment our dreaming mind may reveal the true feelings and urges we mask when awake. There is a real difference between acting in accordance with a virtue, and holding it within us. Over time, enacting the virtue may make it part of us, and again, that's a good process to engage in. Fake it until you make it is a viable approach if your aim is to make it, not to stay in a place of pretence. Faking a virtue for other reasons will have far less productive consequences.

Walking a spiritual path helps us develop self-discipline and self-awareness, if those are things we are looking for. We change our behaviour as our understanding develops; becoming more able to see how to manifest belief through action. As we do this, our thinking also changes. If, for example, we are working with courage, we will learn not to let ourselves dwell too much on any anxious thoughts of failure and doom without at least including space to think about how best to deal with that. For Pagans, a big part of the awareness shift can involve deliberately moving away from consumerist culture towards a respectful relationship with all things.

If we are only interested in Paganism for the dress style and the titles, our dreams may show this to us. Only we, as individuals, can know for ourselves whether our spirituality runs deep enough to be present in our dreams. Only we can know if we are virtuous because we've adopted certain virtues, or are just adept at appearing in a certain way. In working to be more conscious in dreams, we work to take more active control of our minds and deepen our awareness of life. We seek to know ourselves. This in turn gives us more scope to manifest and express our chosen virtues. From here, we can also explore those states between wakefulness and dreaming, when the mind is both fluid and creative. Our fantasies, desires and longings are all open to consideration. Can we bring these into line with our consciously held beliefs?

When considering any activity as a potential spiritual practice, it is important to ask why we want to do it. The self-aggrandizing urges to look good in other people's eyes and feel special without having to make any real effort, do not make us spiritual. These urges take us away from the life of the soul, if we follow their siren call. Thus it is critically important to ask what it is that we want from our dreams. Are we looking for proof that the gods love us? What would that proof mean? Are we seeking scope for wish fulfilment, to compensate for whatever waking life has failed to deliver? Is that a good thing for us? Would it balance our lives? Are we looking to compensate for something that seems inadequate? How do we view the balance of significance between waking and dreaming realities? What happens if we change the balance of how we value these different ways of being? There are no right answers here, only personal truths.

It is always worth reflecting on personal motives, and coming back regularly to re-examine them. If the answers you get are not to your liking, this is not cause to write yourself off, or beat yourself up. Only by recognising how we are and where we are in life can we begin to choose for ourselves. This is a process, not a test we must pass or fail. It is also important to recognise that there is no hierarchy of virtue here. There is nothing wrong with needing escapism sometimes. That can lead us to inspiration and insight, it can give us rest and relief. There is nothing wrong with wanting to compensate for a lack, or wanting affirmation and reassurance.

The only critically important thing in all of this is to know what you are doing. Know what comes from your heart. Name the needs that drive you. It is all too easy to lock ourselves into circles of thinking and feeling that do not serve us. For example, if I think I am ugly, and therefore believe no one will want me, I may not make approaches to anyone. I interpret signs of interest as jokes at my expense. I compensate for this with a fantasy love life and erotic dreams. Now, I can either build courage and confidence from there to change my life and how I relate to people, or I can fold into the safe dream loves, and keep telling myself that I could never have that engagement with a living person. If I'm not fully conscious of what I'm doing and why, it will be far easier for me to let my dreamwork reinforce the beliefs I have, when those may in fact be causing the problem in the first place.

If we are honest about why we need to escape sometimes, we can work with that within our lives, and escape when we need to. If we own the fears, the urges and insufficiencies, accepting ourselves warts and all, we give ourselves a lot more room to grow. We are all flawed and fallible, all looking for reassurance to some degree, we all have bad days, we all struggle with things, fall short of our expectations and make mistakes. If we can be honest about that and know it for what it is, that enables us in our spiritual journeys and life choices alike. Often the most dysfunctional people are the ones most intent on seeming perfect.

The best reasons to explore dreaming as a spiritual practice are the best reasons to do anything. To experience. To learn. To discover. To feel. To be more alive and more engaged with life. To be inspired and nourished. To cultivate personal virtues. To seek numinous encounters. To find that which we love and which brings passion and meaning into our lives.

No one else is watching or judging you. The spiritual value of your dreaming life is utterly private.

Dream Incubation

There is a tale of ancient bards shutting themselves into darkened huts, with a stone on their stomachs, there to lie and incubate dreams. Reports of this run through to much more recent bardic questing. I don't reliably have total darkness and I certainly don't have access to an isolation hut. Thus far, attempting to work with a stone hasn't helped much. I find them a distraction from sleep – perhaps more productive if the aim is not to induce dreams, but to create hallucinations from sleep deprivation.

There are shamanic techniques from around the world that are essentially ways of changing your brain chemistry in order to affect what you experience, and to induce trance. Sleep deprivation, sensory deprivation, fasting, pain and extreme physical exertion all affect the mind and can therefore lead us to dreams and visions. This can also be achieved by imbibing substances. Prayer and meditation will also alter and open us. We mess with our brain chemistry all the time – sugar, caffeine, alcohol and nicotine are the most common methods. In essence, everything we consume and everything we do impacts on our brain chemistry. There are always risks and issues, regardless of whether you're doing it deliberately for spiritual effect, or just being a normal modern human.

Altering your brain chemistry can be a beautiful and magical experience. It can also open the door to demons and disease that have been waiting around all your life. Until or unless you open these doors, you do not find out whether you are going to go insane or become a poet. Or both. Or neither. The general wisdom is that mental illness and deep spiritual work are not good to mix, especially without support. That said, I know people who do just that and who benefit from it. Ultimately, we are all practically responsible for making our choices and actions regardless of whether society would consider us capable of making those choices. Depressive illness and anxiety can be helped by changing how you think. Sometimes we have to go a little crazy and break before we are able to heal. While I would suggest not wading into this lightly or carelessly, life can deliver these changes to you whether you seek them or not. Take care of yourself on whatever terms best make sense to you.

Many more shamanic practices can seem from the outside to be a lot like courting temporary insanity. The lengths that can be gone to in search of vision make it clear that this kind of experience doesn't happen automatically when an untrained enthusiast has a nap. Perhaps the most important idea to take from all of this, is that meaningful dreams must often be worked for. We may receive occasional dreams through grace, but a dream practice is a deliberate approach to working with dreams, an active seeking of dreams, rather than passive reception. The degree to which we do that, and the degree to which we weight dreaming reality against waking reality, is a personal choice. It is a choice that has consequences.

If what we normally do is shuffle carelessly through the day, absorb television content and crawl thoughtlessly under the duvet, it is not reasonable to expect meaningful dreams. If we do not make time for dreams and pay attention to them, we can hardly expect them to provide us with reliable, spiritual experiences. I would also suggest that we need to be reasonably at peace with – in the sense of being in a state of acceptant of – ourselves, or our dreams will simply reflect our unexamined conflicts. At the most basic level, dreamwork is just about paying attention, but at the far end of the scale is a Druid in a dark hut with a stone.

In practice, life throws up challenges and sleep is part of how we cope. There will be times when dream incubation and dedicated dreamwork is not the right response to life. Sometimes we need the dream space to work through what the waking day has thrown our way, and until that's in hand, the rest of it simply won't work so well, anyway. It is not the job of a Pagan to 'transcend' the sore body, the broken heart, the work stress or the family troubles, or any of the other things that can be a tough part of wakeful life. We do not ignore or overcome these things in order to do some imagined 'true' work away in the ether.

All of the work and all of the imaginative play you do, all of the time devoted consciously to life, is part of the spiritual path. Different times create different needs and priorities. There is much to be gained from resolving life issues, and being more at peace with the self and the world is very much the goal of spiritual practice. This is a worthwhile end in its own right and need not serve some other purpose. Sometimes deep sleep is much more important than vivid dreaming. Sometimes processing a loss is what you need to do, and intentional dreamwork has to wait for the heart to heal. We may use our dreamwork to deal with our issues – what we seek doesn't have to be esoteric in order to be valuable. Sometimes the most important work we do does not seem to involve any kind of organised showing up and doing the work at all, instead it all happens unconsciously when we give that space to occur. Often, just being reasonably present and paying attention is all that's required to make changes in our lives. Sometimes, we need to be more deliberate, but often, we don't.

A life lived richly, with care and attention is, by Pagan standards, a life lived well that upholds our spiritual values. There are many ways of achieving this, so there can be no dogma about living fully and living well. Work out what that means to you and do it on your own terms. Living well, fully, authentically and with passion will result in a vibrant and interesting dream life.

If you want to incubate dreams and work with dreams in a

deliberately spiritual way, you have to devote time to it. How you handle that time is up to you. Some of the period directly before you seek sleep will need to be given to preparation. The cares of the day must be dealt with so that they can comfortably be set aside, unless you intend to make those issues a part of the work. Bathing as a ritual act, chanting, drumming, praying, making offerings or meditating might be part of your preparatory work. You might do that earlier in the day, if you find that works for you. It might make sense to work consciously on an idea through the day so that you can carry it into your dreaming. You could walk, or dance, or sit upon the earth. You could go through a ritual appropriate to your tradition. If needs be, more routine activities like cleaning or gardening can be co-opted, although it can take a lot of imaginative effort to change your state of mid while doing something you consider mundane. It is what you do with your mind which matters here, not the precise method you use Reading inspiring material, writing poetry, or painting are equally valid ways of creating a different mental space. Work out what you are seeking, or open yourself to possible experience.

Make time to relieve your mind from irrelevant things, so that you can focus on the dream and your intentions. That doesn't mean repressing things that don't fit the agenda. Techniques to still and empty the mind are of no use at all here. All you achieve by the pushing away of troublesome thoughts is keeping them stashed for later. Give yourself time to reflect on the trivia and concerns of the day. Let your mind wander over what happened. By all means think about the shopping you need to do or the things a friend said online. Pick over the throwaway comment that's been bothering you. If you let these things pass through at their own speed, your mind will naturally clear in its own time, with the added advantage that you have done as much resolving and figuring out as you can at this stage. The more you make a habit of creating this loose, reflective space, the more easily you will get through the things that are bothering you and be able to move beyond them into other kinds of thinking.

Seek sleep with a peaceful but purposeful mind. Once your thoughts are clear of other issues, focus on the material you want your dream to respond to. Use any technique that you find helpful – although I would recommend using techniques you are already familiar with from other work and that come easily and naturally. This is not the best time to try to break in some exciting new way of altering your consciousness. You need your method to be easy and familiar. If you do not have a method of focusing thoughts that you can work with easily, that needs developing first. Something as simple as repeating a clearly worded intention can be enough, but the more visual person may favour symbols, some issues may respond to more narrative visualising, you may use music, scent, breathing techniques, pre-recorded meditations or anything else that you know will work for you. If you aren't familiar with the method then the method itself can become a distraction from getting a relevant dream.

It is often more powerful to simply seek experience rather than having too specific an intent. Try not to assume you know what your answer should look like – in fact try not to imagine there will be some kind of coherent answer, even when you're trying to work on a deeply personal issue and need to resolve something. Take the time to sit with whatever you need to work with. Lie down with it. Feel how it exists within your body. Contemplate it, delve into it, but make sure you hold a calm that permits sleep. If the issue is painful or traumatic, try just letting yourself be aware of it as a presence in your body without focusing on the details of what it is and how it came to be there. It is possible to immerse deeply in this way without triggering painful memory and driving off sleep.

Whatever method you adopt for incubating dreams, seek to dream in an inspired way, rather than just looking for an outcome that would be pleasing. If you ask this of yourself, there is every chance of getting it as an outcome.

Dream Dedication

If you want to work with dreams without necessarily always going to the lengths of attempted incubation, other options are available. A small act of dedication prior to sleep can be very productive. How you go about this will depend a lot on what you believe you are doing, and how you believe everything to do with reality, deity and consciousness works. If you don't have any definite answers to life, the universe and everything, just go with whatever feels most comfortable and natural to you. It is possible to have very vague ideas about the nature of reality and still work with them – the key thing is to feel comfortable. If you are uneasy about what you're doing, then it probably won't work for you.

If you are a theist, offer up your dreaming to the deity of your choosing, or to the idea of deity, if that makes more sense. Make a conscious choice that you are open to experiencing something in your dream, and offer an invitation to touch, inspire and change you in your dreaming. Give your dreams over to your god, or goddess, should they want them. Whether they will do anything with this remains to be seen. This is something you may need to do repeatedly before it has any effect, especially if you do not have a strong relationship with deity or are not in the habit of praying.

If you are a maybeist, agnostic or atheist, you won't have the same clear focus available to you. If you do not believe in anything you consider 'supernatural' this is fine – you can open a deeper dialogue with yourself and simply seek to open your mind. Explore dedicating your dreams to a specific purpose, such as peace, insight or healing.

You may find that the idea of a Jungian collective unconscious appeals to you, and that opening yourself to that is the way to go. You may believe in Akashic records or some other system that makes experience available, and you could explore trying to be more open to this as you dream. You may seek to tap into ancestral knowledge and experience. Dedicate your dreaming to forging a connection.

Wherever you are, the earth is somewhere beneath you and the sky above. If you have a more animist perspective, you may find it helpful to be offering your dreams in openness to the energy around you, or to spirit as you understand and engage with it. Dedicate your dreams to the land, or to the spirits of place.

If you feel strongly that you have, or would like, some kind of spirit guide, then you may offer your dreaming self to them, inviting guidance and inspiration.

It's very difficult to hold secure boundaries and at the same time seek to dream in a spiritually open way. If you go to sleep in a state of openness and invitation, you don't have perfect control over what shows up. You can try to be clear about only welcoming gentle and benevolent things, but your idea of benevolent and how others see that may not align neatly. This is not a perfectly safe activity and be aware that you can end up with an experience you didn't want. If this troubles you, then do not offer yourself in this way. If you invite spirit, deity, ancestors and the like into your dreams you can get more than you are able to cope with. You may get very powerful, alarming, challenging or unsettling dreams. You could get traumatic nightmares. You may not be able to cope with what shows up, you may not like it and it may not be what you wanted. If the possible risks of this make you uncomfortable, do not do it.

I've been working in very open ways with dreams for a great many years now. Mostly it's fine. Sometimes I get nightmares, and on a handful of occasions something has happened that really disturbed me. If you are a more experienced dreamer, you can force yourself awake out of a dream that becomes a problem. If you do not feel confident that you can leave a dream if it goes wrong, you may not be ready for this kind of work. Give yourself more time building your ability to make choices within dreams before you leave yourself vulnerable.

If your understanding of reality includes space for some protective magic, you can of course do that around your dreamwork. Be that a protective charm, a prayer for protection, or an assertion that nothing harmful can come near you, there are options for self protection if you do not want to work in an entirely exposed way. It is worth noting that working without protection is an option, albeit a potentially risky one. How you handle that is very much your responsibility. In shamanic practices sometimes spirits eat people, and tear them apart. It is an important part of the path. The person who is too carefully protected is not allowing themselves to go there – either way it is a choice to make, but sometimes we don't grow unless we accept being broken open first.

What you take into dreaming, is you. If you trust that, and if you are not full of things that are a problem to you, then the odds are you will be fine even if you are unsettled now and then. If you run into problems it is possible that anything difficult that comes to you is entirely needful. However, if you get into something that makes you fearful of sleeping, you need to radically change what you are doing and secure your sleep space. Fear of dreaming is not safe or healthy; sleep deprivation is damaging.

If you get into difficulty, change your patterns and habits around sleep as breaking routines can undermine associations. Use whatever you find soothing or affirming to support you in more comfortable sleeping and do your best not to become anxious. These things can create vicious circles if you let them. Use exercise to tire out your body. Do not use alcohol as it tends to cause more trouble. It is, however, better to use anything that allows you to get back into a good sleeping pattern than to continue in difficulty.

Bed as Sacred Space

Dreamwork transforms sleep into a spiritual practice. Most of us do not have the space to create a permanent dream temple to use exclusively for this work, and will probably just use our own beds most of the time. This has a number of implications that are worth pondering.

Paganism is not about separating 'normal' life from 'spiritual' life, but about seeing the sacred as present in the material world, and honouring nature. Thus making sacred space in our homes, and choosing to use the mundane in sacred ways, is an entirely viable option for a Pagan. Your bed can be your sacred place. There is no sense of disrespect or defiling in bringing the mundane to the sacred. Often what we get from doing this is a deepening awareness of how spirit can manifest in all things, how life is rich with small beauties, and grace is woven into the fabric of existence.

If you share your sleeping space with other humans, or non-human companions, it is worth considering how any change of use may impact on them. If someone else wants to watch films and play computer games in bed, will that work alongside your using the space as a dream temple? How are your own habits going to change in response to the work, and what impact will that have on those around you? It's not honourable to ride roughshod over other people's needs and feelings, even when the goal is spiritual. Impact on waking life is something that needs thought and, if appropriate, tactful negotiation. At the same time, if you need to be able to work with this part of your life and this space, it is reasonable to expect those who care about you to be supportive.

In terms of human relationship, the shared bed can be a very potent focal point for physical and emotional intimacy and for sharing important conversations. It can be a place of closeness and trust. It's also where problems in a relationship can be most visible. Be aware that if you have any issues at all with your bed partner, then trying to use your bed as a sacred space is likely to bring that to the fore. This can be a very productive thing, allowing us to change and grow together. It can also be frightening and destabilising. There are many possible outcomes here. Once you undertake to work in a deliberately sacred and conscious way, things change, and we don't always have much control over what changes or what the consequences are.

This is not a process guaranteed to bring misery, though. Quite the opposite! If you have an emotionally intimate relationship, then sharing the exploration of bed as sacred space can be a lovely thing to do. In that state of increased awareness, your consciousness of being loved and securely held can be increased. The value of that simplest of things – sleeping in the same place – can be celebrated and honoured through the process of this exploration. Bringing a sense of the sacred to things that are simple parts of everyday life is for me, at least, an essentially Pagan activity. Finding the beauty, joy, wonder and potential in what we ordinarily do opens our lives up in so many ways. No relationship is perfect. Where we are working together from a basis of love, trust and respect, the inevitable bumps and falters will be worked through. If any of those essential things are missing, it is better to know this and deal with the consequences.

Using somewhere as a sacred space – be that for ritual, meditation, prayer, magic or dreamwork – impacts on our relationship with the space. Repeated use creates changes in how we think about the space (if you prefer to be wholly pragmatic) but arguably also in changing the atmosphere or energy of the place. That sense of relevance and significance continues even when other things are happening. This can have implications for what happens when we aren't treating the space as sacred. It can affect how others use the space, if they are sensitive to what we are doing. There is every chance it will impact on how we feel about how others use our sacred space. There may be implications for pets, children, house guests and where the dirty laundry goes, to take some obvious examples.

A Pagan sacred space is not supposed to be pristine and it is worth remembering that in any outdoors temple, wild things will show up and take a shit now and then. The shit is no less part of nature. Many of the things around us that might seem to be in conflict with our spiritual work can be re-understood as manifestations of nature; dirt, children and pets most especially. If it does not stop you sleeping, it does not really conflict with the work. If it is in its nature to wake you up (children, dogs, etc) then that is something to flex around. If it is unreasonably demanding, you do not have to accommodate it.

I've found that the addition of plants to the bedroom has made the greatest qualitative difference for me. Even in the dark, when I can't see them, their presence changes things. I am happier when the nights are warm enough for open windows and my sleep and dreaming are improved by being able to hear flowing water.

This working with the bedroom as a sacred space can be an incredibly positive and creative exploration. If you're working alone, or with someone who is sympathetic, then reimagining your room as a dream temple will be a great journey. You might think about layout, colours, decor, altar space, and inspiring images. You may feel no need to make any physical changes at all – which is also fine. The important thing if this is shared space, is to talk about what you are doing and what you are changing. Even if the person you share your sleep with is not Pagan, there are ways of talking about this that can make it accessible and comfortable. That is important, because we're seeking calm and peace, not drama or misery. If your bed partner is not sharing the journey, then talk of meditation and contemplation may be the best way to express what is intended so as to be both reasonably honest and reassuring.

If the journey is shared, then having someone to discuss the experience of dreams with can be a great way both of consolidating memory, and bringing dream experience into life. It can be tempting in shared working to want to find meanings for each other, and it is worth avoiding anything that has any element of competition or authority in it. Our meanings must be our own. The sharing of dreams with someone who is also thinking about their implications can be very revealing of self, and too much exposure is uncomfortable if it isn't treated respectfully. In emotionally close relationships it can be tempting to seek reflections of ourselves or feel uneasy about what else shows up. Jealousy is a destructive emotion, and if we are sharing dreams with partners, we need to accept that they go to other places sometimes. Learning not to read too much into the other person's dreams can be a very important skill to develop.

While there is much to be said for rooting spiritual work in daily life, this often creates a need to change our practical arrangements. Sometimes small tweaks can make a vast difference. Undertaking dreamwork will very likely change how you feel about your bed, and this can in turn impact on everything else that happens there. If this creates tensions and difficulties, it will have a negative impact on your ability to work with dreams, but will teach you a lot of important things about your waking life. Developing a co-operative, supportive space is more important than what colour the walls are. You need to feel peaceful and secure when sleeping, and if for any reason you do not, this is a real cause for concern.

Talking to Your Dreams

You might find it helpful to create or use something that allows you to have an ongoing dialogue with your dreams. You may decide to do this in order to try to focus your dreams a certain way, or simply to bring more creativity and inspiration to your dreaming. You may be working to develop the language of your personal dream symbolism, or to become more aware of dreams in the hopes of dreaming lucidly. You may be trying to break a cycle of nightmares, open up narrow dreaming, or work through an issue.

The tools that we use to talk with our dreams can serve many different functions. You may find that some are more helpful than others, depending on circumstance.

Music on the Edge of Sleep

Going to sleep with music on can be very helpful for relaxation, and breaking the hold of unwanted thoughts. For insomniacs it can help ward off the stress caused by being sleepless. Music can be a way of masking unhelpful background noise, and you might also consider using albums of natural and ambient sounds in this way. Your choice of music might help you to direct your dreaming – you might select a soundtrack that has a certain emotive quality for you, or an association you want to draw on. Be careful that rhythms and words are not a distraction from sleep and also try to avoid becoming dependent on music – if you use it all the time you may find it hard to sleep without it.

As we are in the process of changing our consciousness, it is worth being alert to the possibility that a soundtrack will keep you present in the here and now. Having a soundtrack and then trying not to hear it, working on becoming unaware of it, can be a good way of settling and can help slow down an over-busy mind. Sound readily permeates dreams, so any soundtrack you keep running while asleep may potentially inform your dreaming experience. Waking to music on a radio alarm clock can have some curious effects on dreaming, too!

Oracle Cards

Most packs of oracle cards are beautifully illustrated and any visually appealing set can work as a dreaming tool. Rather than using the oracle with a complex layout of cards at a table, take your pack to bed. Get comfortable in your sleep space and then draw a single card. You might focus purely on the imagery, or also consider the meaning. Spend some time sitting with the card and whatever thoughts and feelings it evokes for you.

This small ritual can be undertaken every night if you want. It has the effect of drawing a line under the day, and reinforcing the shift from waking life into sleeping. The beautiful card will give your unconscious some raw material to be inspired by. Whatever thoughts and feelings the card encourages will give you something to focus on – usually something a bit more esoteric than the trials of waking life. This can help you dream more creatively and will discourage any obsessing over events of the day or sources of stress. You can pick a card at random, or choose something to work with, depending on need and inclination.

As oracle cards always have a spiritual dimension to them, working with them on the edge of sleep reinforces the spiritual side of your life. It is a daily (or less often, if you prefer) reminder of soulful things. If life does not give you much time for spirituality, then this small space on the edge of dreaming may prove highly beneficial to you.

Any other physical object that you can hold, look at or otherwise engage with can function in the same way as an oracle card. You could take a runestone, a crystal, a feather, a wand, or any other item that inspires you. Simply take the time to be with the object you have chosen, let its influence permeate your mind, then put it to one side, turn out the lights and carry on thinking about it.

Regular Diaries

If you find at the end of most days that your head is awash with all that has happened, then a regular diary or journal can be a great help. Writing down what happened in a day and saying something about how you felt, is a process that helps you sort out your memories. It can give clarity on recent events, help you put them into perspective in your life, enable you to release whatever emotions were evoked and to make peace with the day. If doing all of that helps to deal with the day, you may find it easier to settle and sleep, and your dreams may be less preoccupied with sorting and filing memories.

Having a dedicated book and a dedicated few minutes to write in it can usefully contribute to an end–of-day routine. Having a bedtime routine can be just as helpful for adults as it is for babies. We're encouraged to give children a reliable bedtime pattern to help them settle, but all too often overlook the value of this constructed winding down time for adults. If you have a routine, or a set of rituals then you alert your body to the idea that sleep is the next thing on the agenda, and this will help you sleep. It's basically conditioning yourself to recognise that you are going into sleep-time.

If you are keeping a diary of your waking life, it is important not to get bogged down in writing epic amounts of a night – that won't help you sleep! It is also important that diary time does not re-submerge you in drama or difficult emotion. It's more useful to try to look back calmly. Some kind of making-sense process will be of more help to you than re-engaging with intense emotions. If things have been especially challenging, you may need to give yourself more time to reflect on what has happened so that you can then sleep. This is a good habit to cultivate, making us more aware of our lives and more alert to causalities and the impact of our experiences. Taking time to pause and contemplate what has happened enriches life experience and slows us down from the more normal habit of just rushing from one experience to the next.

Regular diaries can be used to informally note any interesting dreams, and there is no reason why you can't record both sets of experiences in the same book if that works for you.

Imagining Your Way Through Physical Practice

There are benefits to body and mind alike of imagining your way through a physical practice. It can help us learn and remember the moves, but there's also a process of relaxing and settling both mind and body. If you practice Tai Chi, yoga or something else of that ilk, you may find it helpful to think your way through the moves on the edge of sleep.

Other forms of physical activity can also be explored to good effect. I find that mentally revisiting the motions of swimming sometimes helps me to settle. I may decide to swim in air rather than in water, as there are no real constraints on how I think about what I'm doing. Walking, dancing, riding, or anything else that has innate rhythms can be beneficial. These rhythms act on our minds, as well as evoking feelings in our bodies, and the trick is to harness something that serves you. If you are going over a dance routine trying to perfect it, that may be a barrier to sleep. If you revisit a gentle walk that you enjoy, it might help your mind to disconnect from your body, walking you into a sleeping state.

I do not recommend focusing on any activity you find stressful or that evokes complex and challenging emotions. However, if you want to work with something that challenges you or takes you into areas of difficulty, the best approach is to allow yourself more time in bed. That way, you can explore whatever you need to and still have time to get enough sleep. Cutting back on sleep to try to work on deep and personal issues is not a good trade off, as the work you do when unconscious will probably be more beneficial than the waking struggles anyway.

You can contemplate physical activity as a way of using edge-of-sleep time to consolidate your physical practice. If your focus is on sleep, it's important not to let any pressures, anxieties or over excitement around the physical action act as a distraction. You can induce adrenaline rushes this way if you work with very exciting activities and, for much the same reasons, meditating on sex can also be counter-productive!

You can use revisiting the practice as a form of meditation. If there are emotive associations that you find soothing, you can use this to help settle your mind. Again, I revisit the motions of swimming because I find the curved shape of breast stroke, the pace and associations inherently settling. Be very clear about what you want to achieve, and assess anything you use in terms of whether it serves that purpose for you. The danger with this kind of meditation is that it becomes yet more work, tying us too strongly to the physical realm and waking concerns, and reinforcing those things rather than resolving them. However, it can serve us well, and it is worth exploring.

Scent

Scent is incredibly evocative, and of all our senses tends to be the one with the most power to impact on our emotions. There's something about smells that seems to come in at a less conscious level, reminding us of things past. We all have scents that evoke certain moods, memories, a sense of place or person and this is something we can harness for dreamwork.

As a practical point, it may be tempting to use scented candles or incense as a way of generating a fragrance. Whatever you do, avoid falling asleep with something on fire in your bedroom. There is simply too much risk of this going wrong. If you really need to burn something to get the exact smell you need, do so when awake and make sure everything is safely extinguished before sleep. Fears of setting fire to the home, or the actuality of setting off a smoke alarm, do not make for good sleeping.

There are a great many scented perfumes and air fresheners you can buy. However, this introduces a whole array of chemicals into your sleep space – something I do not think is a good idea. Artificial scents smell fake, and will not have the same power to evoke, unless for some reason it is the manufactured scent that has the impact. If you want to work with the perfume Granny always wore, or the smell of air freshener from the B&B of your childhood, that's a different issue.

Essential oils may seem more 'natural' but there are reasons for caution here too. These oils can be very strong, and if you put them on your own skin, you may cause irritation or discomfort. Anything you apply to your body or put into your air supply is going to end up inside you, to some degree. Most of us are not biochemical experts, and the best we can do is rely on the familiar not to get us into trouble. If this is not an area of knowledge, you may wish to consult someone with expertise in aromatherapy, or buy essences made by qualified herbalists.

For the less adventurous, perfumes used on the skin, or familiar scent sources put in fabric bags in the pillow case may work best. However, it's not enough to grab a random smelly thing and assume it will do something for you. Take the time to find out how smells evoke memory and feeling for you. Pay attention to what affects you in your waking life, and then harness that to assist your dreamwork by creating and suggesting moods. Spend time sniffing things and considering the effect – by that means you will find out what soothes, comforts and encourages you. We all have different responses to scent, so building an understanding of your own responses is critical for using scent as a prompt.

When working with scents on the edge of sleep, it is as well for many purposes not to use the same scent all the time. We tune out familiar smells. For most of us, 'home' has no smell at all, while other people's abodes will smell strongly of their cleaning agents, cooking, dogs, children and so forth. To keep a smell evocative, it is necessary to keep it a little bit unfamiliar. However, if your only aim is to create a comfortable, sleep-inducing environment then adding your scent of preference to the mix may work perfectly well regardless of whether you are conscious of it. Using the same scent each night might become part of the pre-sleep ritual, and this can be a wholly effective approach.

Once again, what dreamwork offers is an opportunity to find out something about ourselves. Scent tells us about historical associations and sources of emotion. It directs us to very immediate, felt and bodily responses that connect moments across vast stretches of time. That may in turn impact on how we dream.

Making Symbols to Meditate On

Rather than drawing on someone else's oracle images, or working with existing symbols, we might choose to create symbols in order to reflect on them as part of a dialogue with our dreams. There's a whole process here, and it is the effect of the total process that matters, so don't try to cut corners if you take this on!

The first stage is to work out what issues or concepts you want to explore in your dreams. Pick one that you can articulate to yourself reasonably well, and that is also important to you. You can only do as much with this as the issue allows, so if you pick easy stuff and trivia, the results will not be startling. You can use this space to take on the things that are too big, too hard, too demanding and too logic-defying to be sorted out by any other means. Consider the impossible, the unfixable and the unthinkable. Open the door to the things that are normally locked away as being beyond all hope.

For example, one of the things I am working on at present is being able to see the path I should take and having the courage to follow it. That's a shortened way of expressing that fear and self-doubt makes me procrastinate and I am slow to trust my own judgement of situations, which leaves me vulnerable in many ways. I do not move as quickly as I could and so I miss opportunities. I know there are things in my life that have the potential to be hard, demanding or painful and that it will take courage to step up to them. I want to start building the means to do that now. So I need the path and the will to walk it. I need to radically transform myself in order to do this. I've reduced a complex narrative down to two key metaphors.

If you are a wordy person, a metaphor can work just as well as a drawn symbol. Work with whatever best enables you to capture the essence of something. You do not have to conform to anyone else's expectations. If it serves you, make an object, find a stone, write a chant, or a tune. The key is to find a way of focusing what will likely be a large and complex thing down into something small and manageable you can work with. I could of course draw a symbol that represents walking a road with courage, but as I'm not a very visual person, that might not help me much.

Take your symbol (in whatever form it manifests) to the edge of sleep. Don't set yourself up to do any conscious or deliberate work, just go to that space with your symbol. If you have an analytical mind, tend to be a problem solver or an over-thinker, this is in and of itself quite a challenge. Be prepared to have to spend some time getting the hang of it. You aren't looking for answers or trying to reason it out. The odds are you've picked this thing to work on because the reasoning it out and working hard at it approach has already failed to do anything for you.

If you get opportunities waking in the night or first thing in the morning, use them. If you surface with your symbol still in your awareness, carry on being aware of it. Let it be there. Ask nothing of it and do nothing with it. If that wasn't counter-intuitive enough, do your level best not to try to interpret answers from your dreams. Try to do as little as you possibly can, in fact, and be prepared to spend weeks, perhaps even months apparently not doing much aside from lying down with this symbol and just being with it. Change will happen where you cannot see it occurring, but I promise you that this is a means of making change. The more impossible a task you have set yourself, the longer it will take, but anything that is theoretically possible can be achieved over time. I can learn to be brave and decisive and to do the things that need doing without losing so much time in doubt and hesitation. In fact, as I've been working on this book over a year or so, I have made significant progress. I feel more confident in my ability to judge, and more comfortable about taking big decisions. The mantra of seeing the path and finding the courage to walk it stays with me. You can make similar changes.

You will very likely get a sense of things shifting without necessarily being able to pin down in words what is happening for you. This awareness is most likely to come in the edge of sleep time when your mind is flexible and it is easier to feel bold. You can end up feeling more powerful in this time than holds true when properly awake – that's not a thing to worry about, it is simply part of the process. Being able to feel differently at any time will move you in the direction you have chosen. Gradually, you will become able to manifest more of what you are seeking in your waking life.

The only conscious work to be done involves paying attention when awake to any changes occurring. We don't always make the best choices about how to start projects of self change, and sometimes the vision needs fine tuning. What we thought we wanted and what we turn out to need aren't always quite the same. We might have phrased the intent in a way that doesn't work. 'I want to stop being such a fat and ugly cow,' may represent how I feel some days, but that isn't a thought form to enable change. In this example, I would need to face up, eventually, to my underlying issues of self-esteem and my ideas about beauty and body size. I would have started from the wrong place, and it might take me a while to spot that and figure out how to be gentler with myself. Only from there might I do something in my own interests.

You can revise your working at any time. You can create new symbols whenever you need them. Growing and healing show us things we could not have known when we started, and there is nothing wrong with getting to a new vantage point and changing direction.

Extracting Symbols and Archetypes From Dreams

You may find that your dreams re-use symbols and archetypes. A dream diary will make it easier to identify such repeats, but even without one, recurrences can become apparent. You can take these symbols to work with.

A symbol suggests that it must be symbolic of something. However, while it is interesting to figure that out, it is not essential. If you keep seeing a certain kind of bird in your dreams, or a certain kind of item keeps showing up, then you can work with it before you've decided what it signifies. Contemplating the symbol, manifesting it in your waking life in whatever way makes sense, considering it on the edge of sleep, may all bring insights. It may not be a symbol that you've found – it may be an essence, a presence, something in its own right.

You can end up with a dialogue between the symbols you take to the edge of dreaming, and the symbols that come from your sleeping mind. If you lie down with one image, and another one is there when you wake up, then you have to decide what, if anything, to do with that. You may want to infer meaning. You do not have to identify meaning for the experience to confer benefits.

Not all symbols are tidy and easily grasped. It helps to know how your dreaming mind works, but many things can have symbolic function in dreams. You may be more inclined to use actions, setting or people as symbols, than objects. You may use history to reflect the present, tap into books, or express through colour.

I use flight to symbolise how I'm feeling in my soul. Locations and landscapes are really important for me – they are themselves, but they also symbolise my emotional associations with places. Dancing on the tips of my toes is something that I repeatedly do in dreams. I could not manage point-work as a

young ballet student, so this has all kinds of interesting implications. In dreams I do well and naturally that thing I could not
manage at all in waking life: graceful point-work. Why I
sometimes dream that I do not yet know, but it is a powerful
symbol for me. It does not work as a static image – feet in ballet
shoes do not encapsulate it, not least because I normally dream I
am doing this barefoot. The literal dancing on the tips of my toes,
the ease and fluidity of impossible movement, is what holds the
symbolic power here, not the static image.

When looking at dream symbolism it can be tempting to pull
out the things that are most readily described and to assume that
'symbolic' means a visual element that can be translated into
another meaning. Dreams are so much more than a stream of
images. The sounds, emotions and motions of our dreams can
have just as much symbolic value. If you are not a visually orien-
tated person, the key dream symbols might be in the dialogue, or
could even be scents.

The dream symbols we keep coming back to have something
to tell us about ourselves. Whatever we mean by them in the
dreams, we draw on them because they have power, significance,
or emotive qualities. Regardless of whether we try to unravel
individual dreams, we can learn a lot from considering the
symbols we use. They speak to us of ourselves, and it is worth
our while to listen to whatever we are trying to say. The forms
our symbols take – words, images, dance moves, settings – are
part of who we are, part of our inner landscape. Working with
that, we can come to know more about ourselves.

When you extract symbols from dreams in order to work with
them, the only essential thing is to choose a method of working
that suits you. I had a failed experiment into making visual
symbols, and an idea about making some kind of dream oracle
set to work with. I'm just not visual enough. I felt no sense of
emotional connection with the symbols I was making, and it
seemed too much like an intellectual exercise. I gave up on it, and

went back to working primarily with words, because that suits me best. In experimenting, and accepting that it doesn't always work, we have more scope to learn about our lives.

Chapter Nine

Into the Wilderness

As Pagans we seek to connect with nature. We honour nature. We may worship spirits or deities of nature as well. And yet at the same time we live in a fast moving, technological 'modern' society that seems bent on eco-suicide, treats the planet as a disposable commodity and people as cogs in the corporate machine. We cannot function as modern humans without, to some degree, engaging in destructive capitalist society and all its anti-nature philosophy. But to be in any way Pagan in our lives, we have to untangle ourselves at least in part from this entirely un-Pagan way of being. The result will inevitably be a kind of precarious, uneasy balancing act.

Our species cannot go on as it is – there is no alternative to this difficult truth. It can be easy, in face of all that is wrong to just slump into miserable apathy, powerless to make change. We can campaign, protest, vote and even shop our way towards something better. We can choose to re-wild our lives, seeking the sustainable and moving away from the unviable. This is not, to be very clear, some kind of hair shirt exercise in abstinence, self denial and misery. A life lived well is a rich, rewarding life that doesn't cost the earth.

Re-Wilding Your Sleep

Sleep is an innately natural activity, answering a most basic need of our animal selves. It might seem odd therefore to suggest that sleep could need a re-wilding process, but it does. For most of us, sleep does not answer the needs of the animal self, and is more akin to something battery farmed than something free range, much less something wild. Understanding the ways in which our sleep is not wild challenges a great many norms in

172

modern living.

All mammals sleep, and so in sleeping we are connected to them all through shared experience, just as we are connected to all other humans, too. It is worth reflecting on how much is shared, how much we have in common with other living things. In understanding our commonality we are better able to empathise with each other, and to act with compassion. Recognising this commonality is radical, in a culture that encourages us to see everything as a potential commercial resource, including other people. Our exploitative culture creates artificial boundaries; chains of user and used that have little to do with natural food chains or ecological systems. If we see ourselves as part of the world, and more the same than not, we take a step closer to wildness.

In sleep, we are all much the same, and it makes us all equally vulnerable, regardless of species. Our titles, bank balances and worldly goods can't help us much. We are in many ways more real and exposed by sleep than we might choose to be when awake. The dreaming mind is both less willing, and less able to lie to itself. Thus our fears, desires, hopes and motives can be uncomfortably exposed by our dreams. Equally we might welcome and delight in that insight, and we might value and appreciate what we find within ourselves. The shaming, devaluing opinions of others might also be revealed as illusions by our sleeping selves.

When we sleep and dream, we enter a profoundly natural and necessary state. However, it is a mistake to see dreaming as some kind of primitive wilderness, inherently trustworthy, innocent, and separate from our waking lives. We bring our minds with us when we dream. All that we are, know and do, the material context of our existences, our beliefs, assumptions and the culture we belong to will all influence us as we sleep. Our attitude to sleep can leave us with unnatural sleep patterns. Statistics for the UK suggest that about 80% of people do not get eight hours sleep a night.

It might be tempting to see as inevitable the tension here between what is natural, and what is part of civilisation and progress. There is nothing innately wrong with the idea of civilisation. Without it, I could not write these words and no book or ebook would exist for you to read. All that is best about humanity is expressed through the civilisations we have constructed. However, it is equally true that our worst and most destructive habits are also bound up in our civilisations. Greed, hunger for power and control, violence, cruelty, destructive urges – we have hard wired all of these into our laws, politics and habits at various times through our history. Our assumption of a fundamental right to use and consume informs so much of what we do and how we mistreat each other and our habitat.

Civilisation does not have to be at odds with nature and it is not inevitable that civilisation requires us to live, and sleep, in unnatural ways. Not all historical cultures have been at war with the natural world, not all contemporary cultures are inherently destructive. We could construct societies that seek to work in harmony with the natural world. We could choose to favour co-operation over competition. We could collectively decide that quality of life for all is more important than profits for the few. By its very nature, any given civilisation is a construct, and there is always scope to build something different.

To move away from all that is worst about current human cultures, while managing to keep the good bits, seems like a challenging but feasible aim. We need to collectively give up on greed and the desire to wield power. We must learn to co-operate with each other, with other living things and with nature as a whole. Without these changes, we are likely to make the Earth uninhabitable for our species, which is hardly a wise strategy! Thus the personal meets with the political, and the microcosm of our lives is revealed to be a reflection of a much bigger picture. How we relate to nature is intimately connected to how we relate to the nature manifest in ourselves. If we can respect nature within ourselves – for example by learning to respect our own need for sleep, we become better able to respect nature in other forms, too.

To talk about re-wilding your dreams, is to consider changing your life, and by extension the culture you inhabit. If we all change, everything changes. I do not believe in the idea that changing consciousness magically alters everything – we will not save the world by a few of us praying or meditating. However, when changing your spiritual practice changes your day-to-day life, and requires others to question what they do in turn, then there are some real opportunities for radical shifts.

To re-wild your dreams calls for changing your relationship with self. There are a great many things we might do to re-wild, some of which will be explored in the following pages. As we all exist in relation to each other and the wider world, we cannot change what we do without also creating ripples of change in other areas of our lives. Changing our relationship with all that is beyond self, inevitably has vast consequences for the individual. Re-wilding dreams will not put an end to climate change and extinction, but the process of seeking a wilder experience will nonetheless take us in that direction. We are part of a vast web of life, after all. No action can be separate from the whole.

You may well find that it is not currently possible for you to do all of the things that might re-wild your dreams. Any change you make is worth making, this is not an all-or-nothing scenario. Do what you can, know what you cannot do and why, and take that journey one step at a time.

Physical Re-Wilding

Physical re-wilding is the process of making your sleep more natural. It sounds like a simple and obvious thing to do, but in fact is surprisingly difficult because of the demands of modern culture. The most important thing you could do to re-wild your sleep, is this: when you are tired, go to sleep. Only by sleeping sufficiently in response to being tired can we develop natural sleep patterns and ensure we are answering our body's need for sleep. Most of us do not have this option most of the time.

If we are ill, in mind or body, we can need extra sleep to help with the recovery process. The odds are that you can't sleep whenever it seems like a good idea, perhaps not even when it feels wholly necessary. It is worth giving some thought to identifying all the reasons that you do not just go to bed and sleep whenever you are tired. Why are you not giving yourself, or allowed to have, this most basic and essential thing? There will be reasons. Work and school, financial necessities, the demands and needs of others, lack of suitable space, and a culture that gives no priority to sleep are likely candidates.

Consider what would need to change in your life for you to be able to sleep as long and as often as you truly need to. If you can make any changes that allow you more sleep, then make those changes. Even if you can't get the perfect arrangement, it is worth doing the very best you can for yourself, whenever that's an option. If you feel guilty about 'wasting' time on extra sleep, do have a good think about the culture we have that so readily equates necessary rest with indolence.

All the rest of nature relaxes when it can and sleeps when it's tired, and only does otherwise if there's an emergency. We live day to day as though in a state of emergency; no wonder stress, depression and anxiety are at an epidemic level! To be more natural in our lives we must engage with these basic things.

Noise and light pollution are chronic in modern towns and cities. Both are intrusions that can and do interfere with sleep. Most of us inhabit constructed urban environments that impede our scope for taking essential rest. What would need to change for your sleep-habitat to be more conducive to sleeping? The odds are that much of the noise and light you are exposed to are not within your control. Traffic can create a great deal of both, although lower speed limits would reduce the endless noise pollution from cars. Less intrusive street lighting is available, but not a priority in most places. Do we really need this 24/7 culture, always noisy, busy and on the go? Are we getting enough out of it to make the cost worth bearing?

Work patterns force many of us into profoundly unnatural sleeping arrangements. If we want to re-wild our sleep we have to change the work culture so that needlessly long hours, night shifts and spaces where we can't take a nap are not part of the mix, or at least not normal and regular features. Teenagers often prefer a later start and there's evidence to suggest that forcing them up early does them no good at all. Night owls hate early mornings, and those who are naturally up with the larks do not take well to night shifts, but we are expected to take whatever jobs we can, regardless of the impact they have on us.

Obviously there are many areas of modern work where sleep patterns are not going to be respected. On factory production lines, security jobs, the emergency services and many others, the work goes on at all hours. It is more efficient to keep the machines running through the night and therefore people must be found to work the machines – and not necessarily those who prefer to be wakeful by night. A wilder and more natural approach to sleeping would not work for those making a profit out of the sleepless labour of others. We are all complicit to some degree in this system that favours the convenience of everything being available to us most of the time, over the quality of life that comes from decent rest.

It is difficult to imagine what our society would look like if we valued sleep. The changes would be many and wide-reaching. We cannot all re-wild our sleep unless we change our collective attitude to work and convenience. If re-wilding is only an option for the fortunate few, the political implications are considerable. Currently, work and the culture around it define our sleep far more than the need for sleep does. The longer hours we are required to work, the less rest we get and the less time we have for sleeping.

Overstimulation is a modern plague. We expect ourselves to keep up with so much fast moving information and to be incredibly busy. Expectations are preposterously high for many of us, such that just stopping for a little while can seem tantamount to madness. Over-stimulating media can also be addictive – I certainly struggle to break away from it sometimes and find it is still influencing my thoughts long after I've gone to bed. We can be flat out in our work, our leisure, our family lives, always running around trying to achieve things and perpetually exhausted. The idea that the fast lane is a good thing and the hectic modern lifestyle a necessity, is hammered into us relentlessly. To step away from that and just go to bed is a radical political choice. It isn't an easy break to make – especially not at first.

It's worth noting that we don't consume as much when we're asleep – no one makes a profit out of us. We also don't make good choices when we're sleep deprived and are more likely to gain weight – all of which opens the way to various forms of financial and political exploitation. If you had time to stop and think, you might be less keen to run on someone else's treadmill so that you can pay for things you barely have time to enjoy. If you've stopped already, you'll know how this works.

We Westerners tend to sleep in soft, constructed places that are insulated to a fair degree from the natural world. Most of the time this comfort is very welcome, and can improve quality of sleep. It is, however, worth exploring the relationship between the natural world and sleep. What can you hear from your bed? What can you smell? What of the natural world is present in your sleep space, and what happens if you pay it more attention?

It is a very different experience to sleep on the earth, under the stars rather than in a bed. It's a much colder experience, often necessitating a hat, and resulting in lighter and more inter-mittent sleep. Sleeping out can mean being rained on or waking up damp and cold with the dew. Waking up because the fire went out, or a fox called. Sleeping in the warmth of the afternoon sun is a different experience again, and you risk sunburn. There is little that feels wilder than sleeping on the earth without a tent, although most of us will find it doesn't make for deep sleeping. Perhaps if we practised, we would sleep more easily in such situations.

Other mammals sleep together for warmth and security, but we tend to have one bedfellow, or sleep alone. The sharing of a bed is a sexualised activity in modern, Western culture such that saying you have slept with someone would normally be under-stood to mean you have had sex with them, not that you have shared a sleeping space. Children have to be put safely into separate beds because no one can be trusted not to take advantage. Our greedy, destructive, selfish and possessive habits as a culture affect how we are able to share sleep spaces. To be naturally huddled up for warmth and comfort is to court abuse. So much for civilisation.

Our bodies respond to seasonal changes in light levels, and to temperature. We are affected by climate, sunlight and the amount of colour we experience. If winter darkness inspires an urge to retreat, or hibernate, you'll instead be encouraged to take anti-depressants or to use a sun lamp in order to cope and work normally. Retreating into that darkness is not a socially accepted option. We take a similar approach to menstrual cycles, pregnancy, illness, stress and life changes. In face of all the things that make us want to curl up in the comfortable darkness and rest, we instead push ourselves towards chemical interventions, so that we can remove the symptoms and carry on as usual.

We cannot re-wild our dreams while forcing ourselves to ignore our natural rhythms, cycles, needs and life events. All too often what we will find in our lives is that the balance between nature and civilisation is sacrificed in the name of profit. Not our own profit, either. Reclaiming sleep is very much an issue of reclaiming quality of life, and increasing our autonomy. As work increasingly dominates the work-life balance for many people, it is a subversive and political move to seek more sleep. At the time of typing, yougov.com has recently reported on a poll indicating that about 80% of people do not reliably get eight hours sleep a night. Recent reporting on the BBC website indicates that scientists from prestigious universities have linked cancer, heart disease, type-2 diabetes, infections and obesity to reduced sleep. How we allow ourselves to be treated around the issue of accessing sleep, informs our physical wellness. We have a right to know the implications and we really should be entitled to act in our own interests.

Mental Re-Wilding

I am not a mind-body dualist and I do not see the head and the flesh as somehow separate from each other. Recognising that the biology of the mind and body are part of the same system is important if we are to understand what our minds do. These are not abstract computers transcending the concerns of the rest of the body. However, sometimes it helps to distinguish between bodily experience and that which occurs primarily in our thoughts, with no visible, external reality. As body and mind are connected and interacting, what happens to one will impact upon the other. Our thoughts will affect our bodies just as our bodies inform our thoughts. This can lock us into destructive cycles, or help us build more potent ways of being and thinking.

Biologically speaking, we are designed to cope with short term stresses where the solution is either fight or flight. Our entire adrenal system is geared for this, giving us the focus and energy to flee sabre-toothed tigers and hunt aurochs, run away from rockslides, escape wildfires, fend off rival humans and make it home from demanding foraging trips. Millions of years of evolutions went into equipping us to deal effectively with these short term issues. In the blink of an eye on the evolutionary time scale, we've replaced the dangers of the natural world with roads, offices, solicitors, insurance claims, queues, government paperwork, tax returns, exams, inspections, employers and more. Most of these modern hazards are unlikely to kill you in a quick and direct way, but the long term harm to your body can be considerable.

Modern life is full of things that threaten, alarm, enrage, frustrate and distress us. The reality we have all helped to construct and maintain does not allow us to respond to most stresses by fighting or fleeing in the way we've evolved to. Our bodies are gearing up to run, or to hit something. We must stand still, being quiet and obedient while our primitive adrenal glands pump furiously, certain in our bodies that we'll have to take dramatic action sometime very soon. Our minds have to suppress that bodily reaction to keep our behaviour socially acceptable. We know collectively that when this happens continually for a person, it creates the kind of stress that makes us physically ill and causes mental illness as well. And yet we perpetuate the culture that is so harmful to us.

Running away from the tax man and thumping the bank manager are not viable options. However, if we want to re-wild our minds then the impact of normal life stress is an important consideration. If our minds are constantly awash with stress chemicals and we are constantly suppressing fight and flight urges, we might be too wound up to sleep, much less able to dream.

We might offset these issues with physical exertion, which can relieve stress after the event. We may be able to seek less stressful arrangements. It may be that there seem to be no alternatives and so, perhaps less helpfully, we turn to drugs, nicotine, alcohol, sugar, apathy and denial as survival tools. None of this bodes well for our quality of life or for our sleeping. To function as modern humans, we have to pretend that the constructed modern environment is fine and that we have no trouble coping with any aspect of it. Succumb to anger, fear or weeping and you face being labelled as flaky, irrational, or unstable. The more able you are to hide your innate, animal responses, the better, it seems. We understand the mind as a means for controlling the body and suppressing its needs and urges. We are to pretend that everything is fine, and all too often we keep doing that until our minds shatter or we have a heart attack.

In terms of re-wilding the mind, the most important thing is to begin by recognising and owning stresses and all of the other emotions that we have and are encouraged to bury. In letting ourselves know how we feel, and in letting the mind engage with bodily experience of these feelings, we let our minds reintegrate with our bodies. We're no longer fabricating the illusion of civilisation and forcing our minds to tune out everything our bodies are saying. Then at least we have some idea what's going on with us. If we stop using our minds to suppress all of our bodily responses, we move away from a very synthetic dualism and towards a more holistic awareness. Even if you do not believe your life makes it safe or possible to express how you really feel, just having a little headspace where you can admit your feelings to yourself is a great help. Take the time to name it and own it, this really does make a difference. It can change everything in terms of how you are on the inside, and that makes it a good deal easier to change some of what's happening around us.

Owning how you feel is about developing a relationship with yourself, and taking your own experience seriously. It is not about being a better worker, or better able to passively consume. This is about knowing your heart, and becoming aware of your humanity and soul. Once you can acknowledge your feeling responses to both bodily and mental experiences, this may well start to impact on your choices. How can we hope to respect nature outside of ourselves if we do not respect it where it exists inside of ourselves? Our bodily responses are natural, and we can choose what we do with those, but the constant pressure to ignore our most fundamental needs is not healthy.

I suspect we moderns radically underuse our minds. We do not have the complex and intense social interactions of tribe and village we evolved with, and do not depend on social co-operation as our ancestors did. Most of us do not have the survival skills or broad and detailed knowledge of the world our ancestors needed in their daily lives, either. Where our ancestors needed to be capable of doing numerous things, we are used to specialising in a few things and getting the rest done for us. Most of us may well be less skilled and less knowledgeable than most of our ancestors were.

By all accounts, historical bards and Druids committed vast bodies of knowledge to memory. You only need to go back a few hundred years to find that many people were illiterate. That doesn't equate to being ignorant. Historically, most knowledge was passed on orally and retained. These days it is unusual to know a few songs or poems by heart, and we rely on physically storing information in books and the internet, rather than in our minds. We may have access to more information than ever before, while at the same time having less ownership of it or relationship with it. That which is known to us becomes part of us; a very different experience from a quick dabble in Wikipedia.

Amusingly, the story we tell ourselves is most usually one of progress. We are readily inclined to believe that we must, by default, be smarter and better than our ancestors. However, we are becoming more passive in many aspects of our lives. Easy consumption underpins so much of what we do as we become ever more dependent on technology, and ever more isolated from each other. Is ours really a narrative of progress? Might we instead view the 'march of progress' as a loss of relationship, skill, innovation and personal power?

Re-wilding the mind suggests re-learning basic survival

skills. There are many basic things we might well be lacking in and could acquire. Develop a local map inside your head, rather than sat-nav, for example. We could seek knowledge of the flora and fauna, of what it is safe to eat and how to build a fire and cook on it. Our ancestors knew stories and songs, and I am also prepared to bet they spent more time learning and creating than most of us do now. I suggest that re-wilding the mind means becoming active problem solvers and innovators. A wild mind is a creative mind. Re-wilding means asking questions about everything we encounter rather than being complacent.

Children, I suspect, have much wilder minds than most adults. They ask 'Why?' a lot and aren't afraid to voice all the other available questions as well. Children start out with no assumptions about causes and effects. Many of them are, from my experience, intensely alert to issues of fairness in a way that more jaded adults aren't. They aren't all little monsters – *Lord of the Flies* style – who must be tamed. They play, explore and make stuff up, all habits we easily lose as adults. Growing up too often means an acceptance of other people's stories about How It Is and Must Be. We forget to question what we're given and we stop wondering about alternatives.

If we tend to starve and ignore our imaginations during our waking hours, what have we got to dream with? Imagination is like everything else – if you don't use and nurture it, little happens and you'll probably lose capacity. If we do not daydream, it will affect how we dream. Daydreaming and engaging in imaginative activities is therefore an act of re-wilding.

If we are thinking, questioning, learning, interacting, pondering, imagining, when awake, this too will impact on our dreams. The alert, creative and active mind will dream differently from the mind that doesn't care and really can't be bothered. The implications for who we are, and who we might choose to be, are vast.

Matters of the mind raise the issue of how we define 'natural' in the first place. It can be tempting to perceive 'nature' as something at odds with human civilisation and either to prioritise and romanticise the non-human, or to assume our least considered responses must be our most natural ones. To re-wild the dreaming mind, you must first engage with these largely unanswerable questions. What, inside of your mind, can be described as natural? What of your thinking, if any, represents an unnatural construct that needs disassembling? Are your impulses good and natural, by your own understanding of what that means? Or are your impulses savage and irrational? What are you measuring that against? Is this kind of self-analysis counter-productive? Would it seem more natural to aspire not to think, or to carefully avoid over-thinking? There are no tidy answers to these questions, but posing them is helpful, nonetheless.

We are an animal that dreams and that has the capacity for doing so in wild and glorious ways. We are storytelling creatures, capable of amazing thinking and creativity. We are reasoning creatures, attracted to problem solving and delighting in unravelling the puzzles of existence. I would argue that it is human nature to think and question.

How we think about our emotional lives is implicated in all of this, too. I am a big fan of the idea that we can productively think about our feelings. I'm also very aware that emotions, especially the deep ones, aren't always available to be contemplated. Sometimes they are a pull in the gut, an ache in the heart and it takes a long time to ascertain what they mean and where they come from. For a while I may just have to accept feeling them because sense and meaning just aren't available. For me, part of the re-wilding process involves recognising those times when I need to let my unconscious get on with it. I may be like a snake, taking months to digest a whole cow. All you can do when that happens is sit there and trust that, unseen and in the darkness, the digestion is happening. The needful process will occur in its own time. There is no hurrying it along. I have found this especially true around issues of emotional healing.

There is a world of difference here between the inner life and the behaviour we manifest. We can think about and take control of what we choose to do, while being very fluid and uncontrolled in how we feel. We can also construct our feelings with our thoughts. Spend a day telling yourself how awful life is, and you will feel worse about things. Spend a day telling yourself life is good and you will feel better. If the day is awesome you may forget to make yourself miserable, and if the day is shitty you may not have the optimism to transcend it, but on a bland and unremarkable day, what you think shapes how you feel.

This is not to advocate a 'peace and joy or else' philosophy. We do need the other emotions. We need to get angry about injustice, and grieve our losses. Sometimes frustration, boredom and misery are vital spurs that get us moving towards where we truly need to be. Unfounded optimism can be just as damaging as unfounded gloom – it's not just about how we feel, it's about how that causes us to live. If we're looking for our own, most authentic feelings we do need to look at how our habitual thoughts might be shaping our emotional lives. Spend each day telling yourself how lucky you are when in truth your life is killing you, and you'll have some serious cognitive dissonance issues to sort out.

When we come to consider our individual natures, there are even more questions to ask. Who are we, really? What is intrinsically me, and what have I taken in from outside? If we are dreaming with minds full of cultural assumption and internalised stereotypes, we are a long way from being a wild and authentic self. However, if we have drawn other people's ideas into ourselves and been shaped by them, this is a slow process that may go unnoticed. There's nothing innately unnatural about being influenced – we are capable of learning by observation so it is clearly a natural thing to do. But how much can we be influenced before we stop being recognisably ourselves?

We may have been indoctrinated by culture since birth, trapped in constructed identities not our own. How do we tell? We are surprisingly malleable creatures. We can change our beliefs, thoughts and feelings, given time and opportunity. There is no automatic way of identifying one set of responses as universally valid, as being the things that prove we are truly ourselves. There is no absolute truth we can apply to ourselves that guarantees authenticity. However, we are able to choose. The modes of thought, the ways of feeling and the beliefs that we deliberately choose are perhaps the ones we can claim as most natural to us. That which we absorb casually may have little meaning to us. In terms of authenticity, choice may be everything. We can't unpick nature and influence easily, but we can make deliberate choices about the people we want to be, and perhaps in upholding those have the most scope to be true to ourselves.

Re-wilding does not have to mean becoming dangerously impulsive, self-indulgent, inappropriately unboundaried, or otherwise antisocial. If we find we have urges taking us that way, we are able to choose what we manifest. Authentic feeling and ways of living that open us to our own responses are good things, but need not dictate how we behave. How we express our emotions is a matter of choice. No amount of re-wilding relieves us of our responsibility for our choices and our actions.

Spiritual Re-Wilding

Wild spirituality is rooted in experience. It is immediate, lived, felt and expressed. Saying that does not in any way invalidate intellectual or philosophical approaches to Paganism. The wild and the civilised can be explored together, neither precludes the other. Wild moments in the rain or sun can be helpfully framed by what we read. Emotion can be understood and enriched through deliberate reflection. On the flip side, abstract concepts and reason are also much enriched by living out our ideas and engaging with them emotionally. If I believed that thinking was at odds with feeling, I could not have written this book. I do not believe that thinking and feeling approaches are separate or at odds with each other, nor do I think one is more natural than the other. However, we currently tend to be unbalanced, usually in the direction of too much thought and not enough openness to feeling. Too much control and not enough honourable expression. Too much acting out and not enough reflection. Too much structure and not enough wildness. I believe that the best expression of our natures will lie somewhere in the balance between these extremes and that most of us are sorely unbalanced in our lives.

For centuries our culture has been dominated by the idea that the key to being religious lies in a very few books and that we need experienced experts to manage our spiritual lives for us. In contrast to this, wild spirituality is inherently personal. It isn't an abstraction or the kind of path that must always lead away from the world, into the ether. Instead it is about spiritual experience that can be felt in the body, with heart, lips and fingers.

Dreaming is an attractive thing to draw into a path of re-wilding – not because it takes us away from life into realms of whimsy but because, as I hope I've demonstrated, dreaming is intrinsically part of life and very much connected to the body. Even when dreaming seems chaotic or foolish, it has relevance for our lives.

When you are deliberately walking a spiritual path, it can be tempting to want to control spiritual experiences. We want them to fit in with our expectations and manifest in a way that makes sense to us. Thus we construct temples and rituals, write prayer texts and designate only certain things as special and sacred. We create frameworks in which we can experience the spiritual as something that is dependable, familiar and not too unsettling. We give names to our understanding of deity, and sometimes let ourselves imagine that we've got it all worked out. I've read authors who talk confidently about how we plan our lives before birth, or how deity plans it all for us. Every claim to certainty makes me wince because it is so reductive to do this. Small and finite as we are, how can we possibly imagine ourselves capable of knowing and naming the infinite? How can our tiny, creature minds possibly grasp the mysteries of the universe? What a pale and paltry universe it would be if all of its mystery could be unravelled by and contained within a single human mind. This isn't to say that we should not try to understand as much of it as we can, only that we need to be realistic about our modest theories.

What is beyond us must, by its very nature, be greater than we can imagine. Wild spirituality is an approach that does not try to put spiritual experience into tidy boxes. It is an approach that does not require everything to make sense or be immediately explicable. This is not to advocate being open to every batshit-crazy theory out there. Instead it is to recognise that every theory, however bland or colourful, is a theory. Any and every theory humans have is nothing more than an attempt to put enormity into tiny little trays and files. It doesn't really matter what we call this, as soon as we start trying to make our experiences fit a grand plan, we are in the business of reducing them. That's all well and good for science, but as a spiritual approach, it takes us away from the numinous.

Everyone with a theory will tell you that the theory is based on the evidence, but when we're dealing with spiritual things, we take our beliefs, stories and assumptions with us. We interpret our 'evidence' in light of what we already think, and our theory will tend to fit with our existing world views. This is why atheists do not see the hand of God in their lives, conspiracy theorists do not see random accidents and people who do not believe in Hell are not likely to find evidence for demonic possession. We are driven to make sense of things on the terms we've already accepted. To see further, and experience more, we need to let go of what we think we know, and let experience lead our thinking, rather than how it more usually happens.

Writing about spiritual re-wilding is difficult. I am conscious of the profound limitations of using this kind of non-fiction to advocate re-wilding your spiritual path. I ought to be talking to you across a circle of firelight, and sometimes there should be owls calling above us, or the lonely cries of other predators. You should be able to see something of the passion and the light in my eyes. I should be using improvised, feral poetry to kindle a fire in your head with a few sparks of sacred inspiration. However, what we have is a book, and it falls to you to find others who can sit out under the stars with you and share wonder. You will have to discover your own muddy path and the way to walk, dance, crawl, roll, slither and stumble along it.

Re-wilding works best when you mostly have to figure it out for yourself. The more I try to explain it, the greater the risk of my just building pretty boxes of leaves and feathers for you. They might be attractive, but they are still in essence boxes and a tidying up of that which should not be tidy, or neatly explained.

At the same time I don't want to offer you a pathetic cop-out. It's very easy to suggest that mystery is out there and to imply I know it all while not giving you anything to work with and leaving you no better off than you were. Acknowledging the many limitations of even trying, let us explore the re-wilding of the soul. I'm going to let go of my usual style, because the only thing to do here, is evoke...

When your pulse rises and the hairs lift on the backs of your arms, when you catch a scent of something that calls to you... go. Follow the tingles of inspiration and possibility. Follow hunger and desire, so long as it does not call you to possess. Follow the yearning of your heart. In hunger that cannot be sated and desires that cannot be named there are keys to unlock doors that will lead you onwards.

Listen to the places in your body where you carry wisdom. Listen to the soles of your feet, to your loins and gut, to the knowledge of skin and the prickling of your scalp. Listen to heart and mind, knowing they are not the only parts of you ready to think and feel. Listen to the song your cells are singing to each other.

Learn how to see the absolute, unique beauty in everything around you. Learn how to see the myriad connections between all things until it strikes you as a kind of madness to separate them out. Do both.

Love, and give, until you become so raw and tender that everything breaks your heart. Sniff things. Reach out with your hands into the textures of life. Let existence tell stories to your finger tips. Thinks about the distance between stars until you are giddy and must cling to the earth for fear of falling off. Dance. Bleed. Laugh. Let animal noises come out of your throat when words are not enough.

Look for god under the leaves.

Shout the words of dead poets into the wind.

Be lost.

Take risks.

Dream.

Social Re-Wilding

In wider culture we have something of a taboo against talking about dreams. The idea that hearing about other people's dreams is boring, is widespread. More interesting dreams would, in many situations, constitute 'too much information'. Most of our social interactions do not encourage that kind of disclosure.

There is no great mystery in this. Dreams speak of the emotional, the irrational, the unconscious, the animal self and our spiritual potential. None of these things have a place, nor are they welcome, in the vast majority of our social interactions.

Dreams do not automatically confer power or status and we can't readily compete over them by deploying them in most areas of our life. Worse still, they tend to reveal our fears, darker impulses and most alarmingly of all, our true feelings. Most of us very carefully avoid showing these aspects of self most of the time.

What would happen if our societies had more room in them for the genuine feelings of participants? What if we spent less time being told what we are supposed to want (buy) and more time listening to what each other feels and actually wants? What would happen if we felt secure enough to reveal our anxieties and shortcomings? If those around us also shared their fears and foibles we would have an entirely different context for considering our own issues. Imagine such behaviour becoming normal. Just in knowing how common our fears are, and seeing that people around us are just as flawed and confused as we are, we would all experience some relief and comfort. No doubt there would be peace in reducing social competition and replacing it with recognition of our shared, messy humanity. We could do so much more to help, support, encourage and enable each other if we could share the troubles that haunt our dreams.

Now, go a step further and imagine what would happen to our dreaming if we shared experiences in this way. Would our fears have anything like the same hold over us if we aired them and observed that others share our struggles? I suspect the act of sharing would alleviate a great deal of anxiety and isolation, relieving the pressure on our dreaming minds. What would we dream about then? The possibilities that might open up if we reduced anxiety are alluring.

Sharing dreams would lead to greater investment in dreaming. That in turn would help us tackle our awful cultural attitude to sleep and rest. If we valued dream experiences, we would be more respectful of the need for sleep. The process of sharing would very likely impact on our use of symbols, because consciousness of the intention to share is bound, some of the time, to impact on the dream. We will no longer be dreaming just for ourselves. Hearing about other people's dreams and being exposed to their symbolism would to some degree be akin to adding new words to your vocabulary. Some of us are more emotionally literate than others, and in borrowing each other's symbols we may be better able to conceptualise and express things that were previously beyond us.

The sharing of dreams is a very small activity with dramatic potential to create change. Culture is nothing more than the people upholding it, and this is a perfect opportunity to be the change. However, dream sharing is exposing and can make us vulnerable. Perhaps this is why so many of us seem to prefer a paid professional and approaches safely boundaried by medical and philosophical traditions. Only when dreams are associated with sickness does it currently seem acceptable to explore them in depth, and we are all the poorer as a consequence.

Any good Pagan space should lend itself to dream sharing. Dreams are recognised in many Pagan traditions and, in theory, we are more open than average to unconscious, magical and emotional possibilities. Thus moots, groves, covens and circles may be places to talk about dreams. Pagan friends and family members could well be open to less formal sharing, as well.

How do we share wildly in a way that serves our Paganism, and our quest for re-wilding? I think it is critically important that no one has the right to tell anyone else what their dream means. We must all be allowed to own and determine the meaning of our dreams and no one should be given authority over interpretation. That doesn't rule out collaborative interpretation, but at the same time it does protect us from hierarchy and dogma.

Perhaps the other most important issue for Pagan contexts is resisting the temptation to read in big meanings. In most social contexts, dreams will not confer power or authority, but in a Pagan setting it is possible to use them in this way. We all have egos, and the desire to feel important is a temptation to watch out for. The sorts of dreams where gods have sex with you, prophetic messages are given, angel guides speak and past lives reveal themselves could all give kudos in a supportive Pagan circle. Most dreams are more mundane than this, but it does not take much imagination to interpret dream figures as deities and djinn in disguise. Big meanings can be interpreted in, and relevance shoehorned into, the dream after the event. To further complicate things, if we desire this kind of dream, we might create it for ourselves anyway. Dreaming of the gods does not automatically mean that the gods came to us – it may be nothing more than a projection of desire.

A group that affirms your world view is only a lovely space to be in if your world view isn't harming you. If you allow the sharing of your dreams to let you feel like someone marked out, set apart, or better than others, these are signs that all is not well. Feelings of superiority are a warning sign that we may be being misled by our own ego. Also be alert to pressure to conform, and over-interpretation to fit the desires of the group as a whole. We need to balance openness with healthy scepticism, and enjoyment of dreams with reminders of the idea of gates of horn and ivory – some of what comes is pure phantasm.

Honour your feet of clay, and never be ashamed of your mundane experiences or animal feelings. These are Pagan too. It's not all about dancing with the faeries and riding on unicorns. A life lived well on this Earth might not beget the most exotic of dreams, but is no less authentic and precious for all of that. Good dream sharing is about being more human, more honest, open and authentic. What makes it powerful is the scope for going against conventional, competitive culture. The trick is not to let the habits of the rest of society shape how we share our dreams. Instead, we need to let the act of sharing our dreams, be they ever so small, odd or humble, softly change the rigid normalities of the culture around us.

The Re-Wilding of Dreams

There is a great deal we can do to re-wild our dreams by working with our bodies and generally exploring re-wilding in our lives. We can also look at other things that impact on our dreaming, and try to go directly to the dreams for re-wilding work. Making change often works regardless of where you start. There is no hierarchy here, and it is as viable to start re-wilding your life by working with dreams as it is to start re-wilding your dreams by working on your life. We are holistic beings; all aspects of our lives are connected and so if we really make change in one part of our lives, that will have some knock-on effects elsewhere.

It's not a good idea to pick the bit that is easy and assume doing it will fix everything else. Radical change tends to require more effort, but we can put down some roots or foundations with the easy bits, we can build confidence and a sense of direction. We can do the bits that are most comfortable so that the bits that are not become less intimidating and are more easily achieved.

You won't change your entire life by changing your dreaming, unless you use changing your dreaming as a way to progress towards changing your entire life. If we want to stay where we are and are invested in not moving, we are unlikely to move. If we want something that looks good, but never takes us out of our comfort zone, we may perfect staying still and looking good. What we get tends to relate to what we do.

Spending more time in bed will help with the re-wilding process. It's important to try to have at least some nights when we arrive in bed less than totally exhausted. Having time to relax, think and unwind contributes to dreaming. Having time to be a bit leisurely in the morning is also an advantage. Taking time to lie down and rest outside of your normal sleep sessions is also really productive, giving mind and body chance to catch up.

There is often scope for re-wilding your sleeping environment

– an open window to allow natural sounds in, while undertaking to reduce artificial noise can be productive. Reducing the amount of synthetic chemicals may help to make a more natural environment – cleaning products and 'air fresheners' can make for very unnatural and unhealthy smells. Bed linens that have aired outside smell very different from those that haven't. Small differences like these can have a distinct impact. I've found that I do better with plants in the bedroom, but that cats are too disruptive – others find pets a great advantage for sleeping well, so it's a case of exploring to find out what works for you.

Manage your light carefully. If you have bright light right up until you try to sleep, it will discourage you from settling. Equally, waking into manufactured bright light, or having to put on very bright lights if there's a call of nature in the night, can be very disruptive. Softer lighting, or allowing yourself to engage more naturally with the gloom, can help establish better sleep patterns and encourages you into more natural habits. Bright light interferes with how we sleep.

Try not to have a clock anywhere too obvious. My ideal solution to this has been a small travel clock which closes, where the screen can be lit up for checking in the dark. Although some people find ticking clocks soothing, I find them intrusive. Worse still are alarm clocks with illuminated numbers – giving you light pollution and a constant awareness of the time. If you have any trouble settling or sleeping, the presence of a clock face will draw attention to how the time is passing, which can make the disrupted sleep even more stressful. That in turn, will not help you settle. As commented before, awareness of time can be very different around the edges of sleep. If you keep your awareness of time normal, it does not help with the process of moving into sleep.

Sleeping Naked

We need to move when we sleep – this is vital for circulation. I've never found an item of clothing that could be worn to bed which did not twist, tighten or otherwise become uncomfortable while I moved in the night. Skin doesn't air properly if wrapped up in clothing, either, and this is a health issue. Skin that can breathe generally does better, and there are ailments – heat rash, eczema and thrush spring to mind as obvious examples – that can be exacerbated by sleeping in any kind of attire.

In the normal scheme of things, most of us do not spend much time in just our skins. In bed, it is easy enough to make a warm, private space where nudity is entirely comfortable. Clothing changes our awareness of our bodies. It's surprising how much odds that thin layer of fabric makes to our sense of identity and social interactions. Consider for example the differences between hugging someone who is wearing a T-shirt, and hugging someone who is bare skinned in the upper body. Skin is entirely intimate, but we often lose the intimacy of our own skin.

I find sleeping naked to be a lot more relaxed and comfortable, and that it improves the quality of my sleep. I've also found that, if I am bed sharing with someone I love and trust, the casual skin contact that occurs during the night is deeply affirming, and I do not sleep as well when that is absent. However, if being physically available to yourself in this way is uncomfortable – if you are too self conscious, then forcing it upon yourself will not help you. Experiment gently, and push your boundaries slowly. It is a good thing to feel comfortable in your own skin, but we can be exposed to a lot of cultural messages that discourage this.

People who have suffered abuse can find nudity difficult – this is never something to pressure another person into doing. That thin layer of fabric can feel like a layer of defence, a marked boundary that improves comfort. For the person who needs that, it is well worth keeping. If you would not feel safe sleeping naked, then you need to look at the reasons for that. If you wouldn't feel safe nude, then the odds are you don't feel entirely safe asleep even when clad. We need to feel safe, and be safe when we are sleeping.

Sleeping naked is not consent. It is not permission and not an invitation. It is not a justification for anything else, it does not entitle anyone to do anything, or say anything that is not respectful to that body.

Daydreaming

What do you daydream about? Most of us let fantasy, hope and desire into our minds one way or another, although we might not call it daydreaming. Imagining the perfect kitchen, the job promotion, the gambling win or the movie deal is no less a daydreaming activity than building impossible worlds and cloud castles.

The advertising industry encourages us all to daydream in very specific ways. Adverts show us correlations between products and lifestyle outcomes. Buy this car and women will find you attractive. Buy this sugary drink and your child will have friends. Take this package holiday and your family will miraculously all get on. This deodorant will get you a pay rise. This drink will make you look sophisticated. Every time we watch, we are invited to dream ourselves into other homes, with more upmarket friends and a sparkly bathroom. The key to making the dream real, is a magical product. If we can't afford it, we'll keep longing for it, constantly reminded how this one thing will save us and make life worth living. If we get it, we'll look around and see the next thing we need in order to reach that dream life, and the next. By this means we are locked into cycles of consumption and dissatisfaction.

It is really important to become aware of your own daydreaming habits. Even the shortest flashes of wanting and picturing have an effect. With small, advert-led daydreams, this effect can be cumulative, and can undermine your happiness, sense of self worth, and ability to value things. Once you start paying attention to your smallest daydreams, you can see if this is happening to you. If it is, and you know about it, you can make changes – either reducing your exposure to advertising, or working to manage your thoughts differently. Neither is easy, both are possible.

Daydreaming informed by consumerism is not wild, nor will it make us happy. Instead, it keeps us focused on what we don't have and on all the perceived shortcomings in our lives. Wilder daydreaming calls for better material. Investing more attention in the natural world will help us – be that pondering the shapes of clouds or wondering what it feels like to be a fish, or a tree. We can daydream ideal worlds and perfect solutions, imagine the things we want to make and do. The trick is to keep the products out, and not to let someone else set your daydreaming agenda by showing you the palatial homes of footballers and the surgically altered bodies of their girlfriends.

If your daydreams are made of products, then your dreams will be limited too. The dissatisfaction created by consumer culture will permeate your life. If you can break away from this to become more interested in this season than this season's must have whatever-it-is, you will free yourself into more creative thinking and feeling.

The internet makes pornographic material widely available, and the audience for it is huge. Pornography, if we let it in to our lives, informs our fantasies and our sexual daydreams. I find this highly problematic. Porn tends to offer misleading depictions of the human body – gentlemen with abnormally large genitals and women whose bodies have been modified to conform to certain standards of beauty. I've watched enough porn to know that I find the vast majority of it entirely un-erotic. It tends to focus on penetration and ejaculation in ways that do nothing for me. It is emotionally empty, people don't talk to each other in any way I can relate to. Often women are treated as little more than objects for gratification.

I write as someone who has watched porn, written and read erotica, and discussed porn with addicts and devotees. It is addictive. Like many addictions, those who are hooked often have to go ever further to get a hit. A kind of de-sensitizing occurs, taking viewers towards ever more violent, bizarre, convoluted acts. The trouble with raw, no strings sex, is that the emotional engagement between participants matters. The heart of the act, the soul of it, is lost entirely in what comes down to a lot of grinding, sweating and grunting.

Erotica depends on uncertainty, mystery, and not knowing. It is the revealed ankle to the repressed Victorian. It is the searing gaze that promises, but does not yet lay bare. True erotica is charged, electric, engaging, inspiring. The erotica we dream up for ourselves is, by this measure, infinitely better than anything anyone can sell us or give us in a video. To daydream is to speculate, to plot, to long, to ache, and these are all good things. To passively consume porn is to be a consumer and little more. But, it will get inside your head, it will inflict its pace, narrative and priorities on you, and if it does, you will be the poorer for it. Fortunately, as with most addictions, it isn't a one-way ticket and there is an option of coming back to your own dreams, and actual people with warm bodies and open hearts.

Culture and Dreams

Culture is not the enemy of re-wilding. Good and meaningful cultural experiences can make us more alert to our authentic selves, and help us truly engage with life. Cultural experiences can engage us with modern communities, tradition and tribe alike. We can make emotional journeys through cultural experiences, learn empathy and insight. Stories can help us place ourselves within landscapes and eco-systems. When culture is a meaningful expression of human experience, it helps us navigate through our own experiences. When culture exists mostly to make money and distract us, it does not serve our emotional needs.

A great deal of how cultural experiences impact on you depends on the kind of culture you are engaged with. Culture is not one coherent thing, it is many things – some of which conflict with each other. The choice of what to engage with and what to resist informs our experience, but even so, the many different aspects of cultures we are exposed to affect us in a variety of ways. Communities and traditions create their own cultures, as can local areas, and each of these has unique qualities. For ease and brevity, I'm not going to discuss much of the breadth and depth of what's out there, but I am going to divide culture into two forms – passive and active. There are some grey areas where the way in which you participate, or don't, will define everything. For me, this is the essential division when thinking about issues of re-wilding, but it is not the only ethical consideration.

Passive culture comes to us readily and is absorbed with little effort. It does not ask us to do much or think a great deal. Television has long been the main delivery method for passive entertainment, but there are others. It may play to our emotions, but it will do so in obvious ways – the excitement of big explosions and the pathos of dying kittens are easy to evoke. Films that set out to be rollercoasters or tearjerkers are often self announcing in this regard. They don't leave us emotionally satisfied, but instead we can come away from them feeling a bit empty or used. Passive culture can be a lot like fast food – an easy hit of salt, sugar and artificial flavours that does us little good and all too often leaves us unsatisfied.

The way in which we engage here can sometimes make all the difference. You can watch a programme, and then take time to reflect on it, absorbing it deeply and being enriched by the experience. Or you can spend a whole evening flopped out in front of the TV and take nothing in. Some programming is designed for vacant consumption, not everything will reward deep reflection. Equally, you can sit in a concert, or a lecture, and change your whole relationship with reality. Or you can pay minimal attention and get nothing out of it. Or you can find there is no richness in the content and nothing to nourish you. Getting nothing out of our experiences is incredibly easy, and much of our entertainment offers us little more than a means to pass the time. Being an active participant takes more effort and a more selective, demanding approach. However, with intent, many experiences can be turned into something rich and valuable, although some lend themselves to this more readily than others.

Active culture requires our participation. That doesn't mean we all have to be authors, artists, film makers and the like. It's great if we are creative, but active participation does not require us to be originators all the time. We can be active audience members. Live performance is an exchange between performer and audience, where both have responsibilities for making it work. Without a reader, a book is just a lump of paper. Active engagement with what we encounter turns us into co-creators, sharing ownership of the culture, and being nurtured by the experience of involvement. Feeling involved is empowering and uplifting. If we are active participants we are more likely to be inspired and more willing to be changed by experiences.

Good art has the capacity to haunt us. Powerful ideas stay with us. Engaging settings will show up in our thoughts. It isn't always the best art (by anyone else's measure) that shows up in our dreams, but the material that most resonates with us. By night, some of us go to Hogwarts, to Manderley (again) to the palace of Kubla Khan and the mines of Moria. By night, some of us have secret, double identities. How much you engage with cultural material and how strongly you feel about it will inform whether you take it with you into dreaming.

I have, in the past, played computer games, and found those games encroaching on my dreams. The experience of dreaming the games left me feeling a bit hollow and cheated, and this contributed to my decision not to play. That's an entirely personal choice, but I offer it by way of illustration. This is not a question of high art versus the low brow, or value judgements about whether your comfort source of preference is 'acceptable' – it's about what we do with what we get and whether that works for us. If you dream of Middle Earth and treasure the inspiration of those dreams – excellent. If you're stuck in yet another bloody mine, or clinging to a sheer rock-face with yet another dwarf and wondering where your life went wrong, things need to change.

How you feel about your dream content can tell you how your cultural life is working out for you. It may well be that your diet is too poor. Too much junk food and nothing with meat on its bones. Not enough variety. To many quick hits of refined sugar, but nothing you can build mental muscles out of. A rich cultural life feeds a rich dream life. If we aren't making room for the things that nourish us, but are instead becoming passive consumers of material that does nothing for us, we suffer.

For the Pagan, it can be well worth pushing that bit further. Consider becoming truly active, as storyteller, dancer, painter, musician. Find stories about your landscape. Sing the songs of your tribe. Make intensely political sculptures. If something is missing from this world, if you see the need for a certain kind of tale, a new sort of hero... consider that it may be your job to start making that happen. If you can't make it happen yourself, find someone who does something in at least the right direction, and support them. By this means do we get the richer and more spiritually nourishing culture that gives us wilder dreaming.

Wild Dreams

It is not enough simply to want to re-wild your dreams. However, that desire is essential because without it, nothing else can change. Your dreams will not reliably manifest things that are wholly absent from your waking life. If you are thinking about something when awake, you are making it real to yourself.

If you want the wildness to enter in, and if you crave a closer connection with nature, you must open some cracks that create possibility. If you are smooth, certain and closed in yourself, you are not permeable. Being closed and controlled in this way can feel much more secure, but it reduces our scope to grow and change, locking us into a rigid shell. Nothing can enter. Therefore you have to be willing to make spaces, and carve doorways. You have to be willing to change and to let experience affect you enough to change you. If you can find ways to open your heart and life a little, then you make room for something else to come in.

Call it magic, or spirit, call it God or awen, or hope... Call it anything that allows you to open yourself in invitation. It does not matter if your calling seems to be answered with silence. It does not matter if nothing seems to change. Spiritual work is slow, and sudden drama is more often about personal ego than spirit. It is simply your job to call out with everything you are. Dare to yearn for something until that yearning itself is powerful enough to break you open and create a small change that will invite others.

We are like seeds in tight husks or stirring chicks inside the shell. In this state, we can walk a long way on a spiritual path through discipline and integrity. Acting honourably and holding our boundaries, we can nurture a conscious daily practice. We can do all of this work and still find something important is missing. The light of inspiration does not shine on us, much less through us. We've worked on our issues, healed our life wounds as best we can, resolved our conflicts, and made our peace and yet there is no fire burning in the head and the gods do not speak to us.

If you have done all of the rituals, studied all the lessons and read so many books that they all start to sound a bit familiar, and yet you are still hungry and searching... this is because the only way forward is to break. From a place of self-contained discipline, the idea of breaking seems like madness. This is because it is madness. You court dysfunction and personal disaster by letting go of your defences and self-control. To be anything other than perfectly in control of self is to be sick, by many measures. To be broken is a failure, normally speaking.

Taking your dreams seriously will already have taken you some distance away from the 'normal' world. For much of this book, I have written about dreams as logically as I can, treating them primarily as psychological phenomena. Most of the time that really is the most useful way of considering dreams. However, if you want your dreaming to be more than that, there is no choice but to break a little so that something else can come in. You may not get much choice about how and when you break, often it is something that happens to us and we can either try to work with it when it comes, or try to fight it. Be assured that it will frighten you, and it will hurt. If we are ready to make a journey that is crafted by breaking, then when we break, we will work with the experience. If we are not ready, then we will burn those wounds to cauterize them if we have to and do whatever it takes to stay conventionally whole.

If you are thinking about how powerful and important you can become when you've mastered this new technique, stop. Go back to some of the simpler work. You are not ready to break well and as a consequence you either won't be able to break open, or you'll court pain that you will find yourself unable to work with. Neither is of any great use, but sometimes we go through cycles of these things before we are able to do it well. If the prospect of breaking frightens you – that's fine, and entirely sane. Choose to continue, or choose not to. Either way there will be a path to walk.

Every time I've broken, I have imagined I could not go any further or be more open. Every time so far, I've turned out to be wrong about that. Once you are on this path, I do not think it has an end point. It is always possible to be more open, more able to love, and more able to feel. There is always room for more inspiration, although all bets are off as to whether that will turn you into a poet, a lunatic, or both.

You do not get power by living in this way but you do get a much richer and more involved sense of relationship with all things. You don't always get much say about what gets in, but you can decide how you let it affect you. This is not akin to a climb up a flight of stairs, either. There is no tidy, linear progression in this sort of way of being. There are long, dark crawls underground, paths through enchanted forests, glorious vistas and sudden, unexpected plummets. There is scope to fall in love with everything, and everything gets opportunity to break your heart. That doesn't mean you have to be some sort of masochistic doormat, lying about to be trampled on by all and sundry. Once you start to live in this way, other people's mean spiritedness can do little more than bruise you. It is not pain that will break you repeatedly, but love, and the more you let it flow through you, the more it will open you to increase that flow.

The more deliberately I walk this path, the richer and more affecting my dreams become. The more I reflect on my dreaming experiences, the more I daydream and imagine, the more fluid my whole sense of reality gets. As a consequence I find it easier to empathise, and to imagine my way into other perspectives. There are times when I am almost rendered immobile by my sense of the sacred and there are days when I can't see it at all, which may be as well in terms of my overall ability to function as a person.

The more I allow myself to be myself and to engage wholeheartedly with my life, the more this reflects in my dreaming experiences. The more open my heart is, the less narrow my dreams become. In the past, I became closed down by rather banal cruelty to the point of barely dreaming at all. Learning to open my heart again after that experience has taken some time.

These are not experiences I am inclined to try to use as a basis for generalisation. We each have unique experiences of life and dream. Once we've got to grips with the more basic concerns, the doors into mystery open more readily. I do not know what you will find on the other side of your doors. It is not mine to know. What matters is your own journey, which you can only understand on your own terms.

In Conclusion

It is in the nature of dreams to be both elusive and mysterious. Sometimes, no matter how we seek them, they do not manifest. Sometimes they slip away on waking, leaving tantalising hints and no substance. A dreamworker will not gain total control over their dreaming, nor will their dreams always be magical or significant.

Dreams can give us insight, enrich our lives and bring us wonder. They are a part of life and natural, animal experience and as such they are not an alternative to life or some kind of fantastical escape, but a very real part of our experiences. Even so, the dreamworker must find balance between dream, vision, fantasy and more mundane wakefulness. It is useful to be alert to the differences between different ways of being so that delusion does not creep in, so that we can manage the mundane bits and also prevent the mundane bits from smothering the magic.

To work with dreams is not to practice the kind of magic that leads to definite outcomes. It is not spellwork or prayer. This is an act of opening to the unpredictable, seeing what you can get and then trying to make sense of it, or not, as you prefer. It is worth considering that any meaning might only exist because we choose to perceive it. In terms of our lives, the meanings we give to things are greatly important and influential. The meanings we choose become real for us.

If it is truly the case that dreams are nothing more than the products of our minds, they are no less wondrous and magical for that. How amazing life is, if it can create such strange and inspiring things as dreams! How remarkable are we, if what we are doing is finding useful meaning in the white noise created by our resting brains!

Or perhaps the universe whispers to us as we sleep. Perhaps it is consciousness that begets physical reality, and not the other way round. Perhaps the gods of dreaming carry us into other-worlds. Perhaps we enter the collective unconsciousness, the ancestral memories, or parallel universes.

None of these explanations is any less miraculous than any of the others.

Acknowledgements

No book is written in isolation, and every book is shaped by its author's tribe. I'm blessed in coming into contact with some amazing people, some of whom have become dependable presences. I'm very grateful to everyone who shares the journey and whose writing, ideas, life paths and inspiration shapes me.

Even so, there are a number of people without whom this book would not have happened, and who deserve mentions and my deepest gratitude. I must particularly thank psychoanalyst Frank Malone, who pointed me at the needed Freud content, and James Nichol who straightened me out a bit on the subject of Jung (any mistakes are mine), loaned me a lot of books and helpfully directed me to tighten up a number of weak points in the first draft and to trust my own judgement.

Three people have quietly and soulfully taught me a great deal about breaking, and how to do that well. JJ Middleway has, by example, taught me so much about open heartedness, and Theo Wildcroft set me on the path of re-wilding some years ago. Andrew Wood's artwork also changed my dreaming mind and inspired me to think about actual dream temples at a critical point in the book's development.

Helen Conway's reassurance that the early drafts made sense helped me keep going, and John Conway dropped much needed inspiration into the pot, alerting me to things I had missed and needed to add.

My splendid editor, Trevor Greenfield of Moon Books, generally keeps me inspired and motivated, and the wider Moon Books community is always a source of encouragement. The many people who visit www.druidlife.wordpress.com keep me believing there is a point in what I do, while also keeping my feet firmly on the ground. To the Auroch Grove and the Contemplative Druids, and all the other Druids and Pagans in my wider tribe, much gratitude.

Thank you to my cover art team at Druid camp: Theo and Tom painted me, James Colvin put flowers in my hair, Bish took photographs, Tom did a lot of work in Photoshop. This is the kind of book cover that can only happen with a lot of support, both practical and emotional. It was a big journey for me.

Most of all I must thank Tom Brown, for the hand holding at every awkward bend in the journey, the inspiration, comfort, support (moral and otherwise) and the belief in me. And most of all, for the safe space in which to dream.

Endnotes

1 Bruno Bettelheim, *Freud, & Man's Soul*
2 Michael Foucault, *The History of Sexuality*, Penguin 1984

Moon Books invites you to begin or deepen your encounter with Paganism, in all its rich, creative, flourishing forms.